The Mind of the Scientist
Michael Hoskin

TAPLINGER PUBLISHING COMPANY
New York

First published in the United States 1972 by
TAPLINGER PUBLISHING CO., INC.
New York, New York

Published simultaneously in the Dominion of Canada
by Burns & MacEachern Ltd., Ontario

Library of Congress Catalog Card Number: 72-164020

ISBN 0-8008-5248-6

Contents

Acknowledgement is due to the following for their permission to reproduce illustrations in this book:

Gabinetto Fotografico, Florence, 29 (top); Radio Times Hulton Picture Library, 95 (bottom), 96; Ronan Picture Library, 15, 17, 21, 30, 33, 47 (top), 71, 72, 73, 75 (bottom), 83, 95 (top), 98 (top), 117, 120 (bottom right), 121 (bottom); Royal Astronomical Society, London, 74, 76; Science Museum, London, 50 (bottom); Wellcome Institute of the History of Medicine, 101, 119 (bottom), 120 (top and bottom left), 121 (top).

Preface

Some years ago, Mr John Freeman conducted a series of interviews on BBC television under the general title 'Face to Face'. These interviews were so illuminating that I took them as my model when I was invited by the BBC to prepare five programmes for schools on the history of scientific ideas. After all, Galileo himself used the literary form of an imaginary conversation in order to present to the world many of his most profound scientific insights, and today 'oral history' interviews are routine for historians studying the work of men still living.

In each of these five discussions we imagine our subject, at a point in his life when most of his ideas have been formulated, placed in a television studio with a modern historian of science. Our purpose in interviewing him is to explore the mode of thought he used, the prejudices under which he laboured, and the mistakes he made; but I have tried to clothe these conceptual issues with a human personality, as though he had lived on into the era of videotape. In preparing the scripts I was careful to put into the subject's mouth only sentences which paraphrase those we find in his own writings, or which express views for which there is some other historical justification; in fact, had this book been intended for scholars, every passage would have contained references to documentary sources. It was a pleasure to find my producer, Mr John Cain, as anxious as myself not to compromise historical standards, and the long periods of rehearsal were frequently transformed into seminars in the history of science.

To act the part of oneself is not as easy as one might think, and I owe an enduring debt to Mr Cain and to the five distinguished actors for masking my deficiencies so patiently. I am grateful also to two Cambridge colleagues, Dr D. T. Whiteside for advice on the interview with Newton and Dr R. M. Young for similar help with Darwin.

MICHAEL HOSKIN

Galileo: *Mathematics and nature*

History is written by historians. On any day, in any town, a great number of incidents take place. Of only a few of these is any record kept – the happenings, for example, which are reported in the newspapers. These are the ones which are available to the historian, and from these he must create his history; for him the rest might as well never have happened.

But except for remote times (for the study of which we may have to draw on every scrap of surviving evidence) the selection of facts of historical value does not stop here. Usually the historian must ruthlessly pick out of the vast mass of facts available to him those few which he will use as pegs on which to hang his explanations. In other words, it is true that historical writing is based ultimately on what actually happened, but on only a tiny part of what happened, and even that part has been refracted through the mind of the historian.

Why begin a note on the life of Galileo Galilei with remarks on the nature of history? Because the Galileo of historians of fifty years ago is very different from the Galileo we know today. Earlier historians emphasised the role of experimental facts in science, and their Galileo was essentially a man who looked for facts. The legend of his dropping weights from the Leaning Tower of Pisa summed up their picture of the man: someone who asked questions of nature rather than of Aristotle. Of course there is some justice in this picture. Galileo was quite exceptionally alert to the world around him, and noticed things in a way a modern laboratory-scientist often does not. And he was very clever with his hands. But he seldom if ever performed elaborate experiments as we know them, and usually he asks us to imagine what *would* happen *if* we were to do such and such. For he believed that the mind alone can often give us the answer if we think hard enough; in other words, his achievement was essentially an *intellectual* dissection of nature.

He was born in 1564. His father was a cloth merchant of Pisa, and in 1581 Galileo began his medical studies at the university there. An argumentative pupil, he proved unpopular with his teachers, and he soon tired of medicine in favour of mathematics. In 1589 he was appointed professor of mathematics, but after only three years he transferred to the University of Padua, which lay in the Republic of Venice. There he spent the happiest period of his life, and although he published little it was then that he laid the foundations of his great work in mechanics. But the call of his native Tuscany was too great, and in 1610 he returned to Florence as Chief Mathematician and Philosopher to the Grand Duke.

The previous year word had reached him that in Holland a combination of lenses had been devised to make distant objects seem near, and it was not long before he had worked out a rough theory of how this could happen and had set to work to build telescopes of his own. Whether or not he was the first to use a telescope to study the stars, his little book *The Starry Messenger* (1610) was written with such debating skill that it caused an immediate sensation. Galileo's spy-glass was the forerunner of all the complex scientific apparatus we use today to extend the powers of our senses, and he made the very best of his opportunity to cause trouble for the Aristotelians and to answer objections that had been brought against Copernicus' theory that the Earth moves round the Sun. But Galileo's skill in controversy was too great for his own health. He made many enemies, who attacked him in the most dangerous way by creating an ecclesiastical scandal, claiming that Scripture showed that the Earth is at rest.

Soon the matter was raised at Rome, and Galileo against all advice insisted on going there in person to argue his case. Before long everyone was discussing Copernicanism, as well as the broader questions of the nature of scientific certainty and the relationship of science and religion. Eventually the Pope himself intervened by asking for an official opinion on the motion of the Earth, and in the siege-mentality of the Counter-Reformation the traditional view was upheld: Galileo must no longer defend his doctrine. He turned his energies to less dangerous topics. But in 1623 his old friend Maffeo Barberini was elected Pope Urban VIII, and before long Galileo was being received in frequent audiences. Although the earlier decision was not to be reversed, Galileo understood that he might at least discuss the matter in print, and in 1625 he began the work which was to be published seven years later under the title *Dialogue on the Two Great World Systems*. It is in the form of a discussion between friends, and Galileo wrote it in Italian rather than academic Latin.

At last the astronomers, philosophers and theologians who had suffered under the lash of Galileo's pen saw their opportunity. He was accused of violating the earlier injunction not to defend Copernicanism, compelled to recant, and condemned to permanent house-arrest. In his disgrace, and in spite of his age and rapidly deteriorating health, he turned to a work that had been maturing in his mind ever since his days at Padua. It was published in 1638 as *Discourses on Two New Sciences*, and was his greatest achievement. In it he shows how to apply mathematics to nature and particularly to moving bodies, and why this programme is full of power and promise: the book marks the beginning of modern mathematical physics. Four years later he was dead.

He is now an old man; his eyesight is poor and his health is failing. He is tired, a little bitter at times, and frustrated at his enforced retirement. But when stimulated by conversation he quickly shows the characteristics so well known in the court of Tuscany in earlier years. He is still an intellect of piercing intelligence and dangerously gifted as a controversialist; a poet and connoisseur of beauty; a lover of wine, women and song; a good and loyal friend, if inclined to dominate any company rather too easily – but an enemy to beware. His hands are restless – in fact he is chipping away at a piece of glass while he talks. He is inclined to set about instructing any visitor by putting systematic questions to him in a manner that would be patronising were it not for his patent honesty and love of truth. When the talk turns to topics dear to his heart he shows the vigour of a young man and he is roused by the thought of battles of old, though by now he has learned to smile about them and even to show some sympathy for his opponents' views. We are meeting a highly colourful personality whose faults are easily forgiven by his friends, if not by his too-numerous enemies.

Hoskin: If you read a scientific paper, you might think it had been written by a machine rather than a man. 'Such and such a piece of apparatus *was* taken . . . such and such experiments were performed.' It all sounds so inhuman. You never hear of the confusions, the false trails, the disappointments, the things that went wrong, the rows over who thought of what first, the struggles to get money for that new piece of apparatus.

But scientists are human beings, and science is a creative human activity, not so very different from other creative activities like art and poetry and music. Of course most scientific work is humdrum and routine; but then so is most novel-writing, and we all know how many hours practice the concert pianist must put in each day. Yet occasionally the scientist, like the artist, experiences the deep satisfaction of creating something: a piece of sculpture, or a new theory. And into this new theory the scientist contributes something of himself, something of his inner conviction about what the world is like, a conviction that must always go far beyond the evidence. But it is a big mistake to think of scientific knowledge as simply lying around waiting to be picked up. The scientist chooses which questions to ask, what kind of answer he will accept, which experiments he will make, which facts he will take into account. For all of us, most of the time, these choices are automatic; we have been trained in science, shown examples of what our teachers consider to be good science, and we are told that it is our job to go and do likewise. But from time to time a scientist puts on new spectacles and takes a fresh look at the world, and perhaps he may even succeed in changing the questions and the methods and the kind of answers that are taught to the next generation of scientists. Such men are exceptional, but they are to be found today as in every period.

In each of these five discussions I shall be talking to one of the really great scientists of the past, and I shall try to get him to explain why he looked at the world the way he did, why he asked some questions rather than others, and how he tried to answer them.

My first guest is Galileo Galilei. He lived in Italy in the troubled and glorious time of the Renaissance. His father was an accomplished amateur musician and Galileo himself was endowed with many talents and loved life in all its aspects. He grew up in Pisa and Florence. He trained first in medicine, but later he changed to mathematics and natural philosophy. For many years he taught in the University of Padua, but in 1610 went back to Florence as chief mathematician and philosopher to the Grand Duke.

Galileo wrote a lot and talked a lot, and I think a conversation with him would go something like this: Signor Galilei, I was reading a book recently where the author was discussing the argument you had over how bodies fall when dropped from a height . . .

Galileo: When I was a young professor at Pisa.

Hoskin: He writes that 'the famous experiment of the Leaning Tower was carried out, the blind followers of the ancients were confounded, and a new era in science and thinking was inaugurated'.

Galileo: Sounds like a nice fellow. But what does he mean by science?

Hoskin: Science is the study of the working of nature.

Galileo: Oh, you mean 'natural philosophy'. In that case I should like to think that I *have* inaugurated a new era in science. But surely this man can't think I did it just by climbing up the Tower of Pisa one morning! This science of yours can't be as trivial as that. Besides, I'm afraid that at the time I thought that bodies of different materials could fall at different speeds.

Hoskin: I imagine the writer was thinking of the way you put your theories to the experimental test.

Galileo: But anyone could read of similar experiences carried out a thousand years before my time – though these don't make much impression on the Aristotelians.

Hoskin: Who are the Aristotelians?

Galileo: Men who think to learn the ways of nature by reading the work of Aristotle fifty times!

Hoskin: Rather than finding things out for themselves by experiments.

Galileo: Yes. But the trouble is that all too often the Aristotelians seem to have experience and common sense on *their* side. Look at the amazing strength of mind Copernicus had to show when he asserted that the Earth is rushing along in its path about the Sun. Could anything seem more contradictory to the evidence of our senses? Do we *feel* as though we are racing along at great speed?

And take another example: the Aristotelians taught that the shape of a body helps to determine whether it floats or sinks. They would take some heavy ebony in the shape of a ball and put it into water, and down it would go. But the same wood cut flat would stay on the surface.

Hoskin: By what we call 'surface tension'.

Galileo: Call it what you like, these experiences of theirs made it seem that nature was on their side. I had a very embarrassing time one day when they publicly challenged

The medieval world picture. At the centre (though *not* in the place of honour) are the spheres of earth and water, surrounded by spheres of air and fire. Working outwards in the heavens, we find in turn the spheres of the Moon, Mercury, Venus, the Sun, Mars, Jupiter, Saturn, the starry firmament, the crystalline sphere. the First Mover, and the Abode of God and the Elect. From Petrus Apianus, *Cosmographia*, edition of 1539

me either to dispute with them or to give a practical demonstration to back up my claims.

Hoskin: So what did you do?

Galileo: Well, I just had to refuse, because *they* could produce experiences to back up their arguments, whereas I could not. So I crawled away to write a book on just *why* their experiences seemed to work when I was convinced they shouldn't. But deeds always speak louder than words, and I knew I must try and devise experiences of my own to beat theirs.

Eventually I thought of this one: I took a cone made of wax with enough iron filings in it to make it a little heavier than water . . .

Hoskin: So that if you dropped the cone into water it would sink.

Galileo: Yes, only I didn't drop it in, I put it in very gently, sharp end first. Now remember, the cone is only a *little* heavier than water. Let's pretend you're an Aristotelian. What would you *expect* to happen?

Hoskin: Well, because the pointed end is downwards the cone's shape is ideally suited to pierce the water; and so I sup-

pose an Aristotelian would have to say that the cone would
sink.

Galileo: Exactly so. But my experience proved, in fact, that the
cone floats. Now, what would happen if I then dried the
cone and put it back into the water pointed end upwards?

Hoskin: I suppose an Aristotelian would expect it to float because
the flat base is quite unsuitable for piercing the water.

Galileo: Full marks. But what occurs is exactly the opposite of
what the Aristotelian theory predicted; the cone in fact
sinks. Don't imagine, though, that I just stumbled on this
experience by accident. I did a lot of hard thinking first,
and the experience came later.

Hoskin: You keep saying 'experience' where we would speak of
'experiment'.

Galileo: How do you distinguish them?

Hoskin: Well, experience we acquire as we go about our daily
lives. You might say that experiences come our way of
their own accord. But experiments are artificially con-
trived. Your English contemporary Francis Bacon made
a rather grim joke of it when he spoke of putting nature
to the question – stretching nature out on the rack and
forcing answers out of her. In experiments we make
nature perform under the conditions *we* impose.

Galileo: Yes, yes, excellently put. And just because we are putting
questions to nature we have to decide in advance what
language she speaks.

Hoskin: And what language does she speak?

Galileo: Nature speaks the language of mathematics: the book of
the universe is written in triangles, circles, and other
geometric figures without which it is humanly impossible to understand a single word of it. Plato taught us
this long ago.

Hoskin: Is this why experiments should involve measurement?

Galileo: How easy and obvious this must seem to you now! But
the Aristotelians look at the world in a different way
altogether.

Hoskin: You mean one that doesn't involve mathematics?

Galileo: Yes. They believe the world is a cosmos in which there is purpose and organisation, a kind of large-scale version of a living body where the heart and the liver and the eyes and the feet are all different but all have their parts to play in the total activity of the body. In the same way each stone and each dog and each plant has, according to the Aristotelians, its natural place in the scheme of things. For example, heavy bodies *belong* at the centre of the world.

Hoskin: Which for them is the centre of the Earth.

Galileo: And so if I give this piece of heavy material half a chance it will move so as to get nearer to its proper place – watch (*drops key*). And light bodies, such as a flame, move away from the centre, again, by their very nature.

Hoskin: So that to explain motion involves for an Aristotelian a discussion of the natures of the bodies involved, and of how they relate to the cosmic organisation.

Galileo: Just so.

Hoskin: And therefore mathematics cannot tell us everything about moving bodies, because mathematics knows nothing of proper places and natures trying to get there.

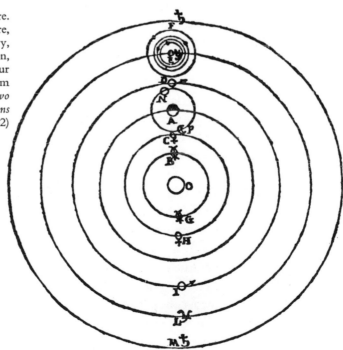

Galileo's world picture. The Sun is at the centre, surrounded by Mercury, Venus, Earth and Moon, Mars, Jupiter (with four moons) and Saturn. From *Dialogue on the Two Great World Systems* (1632)

But surely mathematics can at least tell us something about *how* bodies move.

Galileo: An Aristotelian wouldn't admit even to this. You see, he might argue that in geometry a tangent plane touches a sphere at a single point, whereas a real ball resting on a real table has a whole little area in contact and not just a single point.

Hoskin: In other words, the theorems of mathematics simply do not apply to a physics of the real world.

Galileo: That's what they say, but you try telling them that when you give them short change!

Hoskin: And if mathematical theorems do apply to the real world, they tell us *how* bodies move but nothing about the fundamental question of *why*. I must admit that there I can see some force in their complaint.

Galileo: For centuries the Aristotelians had been writing volume after volume on the subject of motion, and yet no one had more than the vaguest idea on how this simplest of all natural motions takes place. Now consider my mathematical account of how bodies fall!

Hoskin: But surely people had used mathematics to study nature before? In optics, for example?

Galileo: And don't forget the astronomer.

Hoskin: Yes, but I can see that the heavens positively invite the use of mathematics. After all, we actually *see* points of light, and circles in the Sun and Moon, and regular cycles of days and months and years.

Galileo: Yes. And don't forget the work of the superhuman Archimedes. You know, I never mention him without a sense of wonder at the power of his mind.

Hoskin: But didn't he confine himself to bodies at rest?

Galileo: Yes. But he understood so well the problems that face us when we try to relate the ideal world of mathematics to the real world in which we live. We *have* to idealise, because we can't hope to represent mathematically the full richness and complexity of our world – not even if we forget about colours and smells and concentrate on things like shapes and speeds. This means that we must simply forget about anything that's not essential for our purposes.

A page from an edition of the works of Archimedes published in Basel in 1544. The development of printing encouraged the preparation of scholarly editions of such complex and sophisticated mathematical works, which could be studied in manuscript only with extreme difficulty; and these editions in turn did much to stimulate new developments in mathematical physic.

ARCHIMEDIS CIRCV-
LI DIMENSIO.

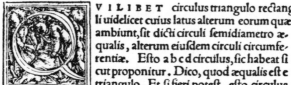

VILIBET circulus triangulo rectangulo æqualis est, il- 1 li uidelicet cuius latus alterum eorum quæ rectum angulum ambiunt, sit dicti circuli semidiametro æqualis, alterum eiusdem circuli circumferentiæ. Esto a b c d circulus, sic habeat si cut proponitur. Dico, quod æqualis est e triangulo. Et si fieri potest, esto circulus dicto triangulo maior, & inscribatur circulo quadratum a c, & diuidantur arcus per æqualia, ducanturǫ ad puncta diuisionum lineæ rectæ, fiantǫ hoc modo intra circulum figuræ rectilineae, donec inciderimus in aliquam figuram rectilineã, quæ sit maior dicto triangulo : & ponatur centrum n. & sit super unum latus figuræ perpendicularis n x. igitur n x est minor latere trianguli. Est etiam linea claudens figuram, minor reliqua trianguli linea, cum sit minor circuli limbo. Dicta igitur figura minor est dicto triangulo: quod quidem absurdum est. Esto item si fieri potest, sit triangulo circulus minor, & circulo circumscribatur quadratum, & arcus inter puncta côtingentiæ circuli interclusi in æqua diuidantur, & per puncta diuisionum ducantur lineæ contingentes. rectus igitur angulus à lineis o a r ambitur, quare o r erit maior r m. nã r m, r a sunt æquales, & triãgulus r o p est maior figura o f a m ǭ dimidium : quare & maior dimidio eius partis quadrati circulo circumscri pti, quæ est ex parte o. Sumptæ sint itaǫ portiones similes ipsi p f a, quæ sint minores eo, quo triangulus e superat circulum a b c d: atque idcirco ipsa quoque figura rectilinea circulo circumscripta, minor erit triangulo e. quod item absurdum est. nam maior esse probatur : quia n a æqualis est perpendiculari trianguli, limbus uero dictæ figuræ base trianguli maior habetur. quare circulus dicto triangulo erit necessario æqualis.

PRoportio cir culi cuiuscũ que ad quadratũ suæ diametri est, sicut undecim ad quatuordecim. Esto circulus, cuius diametrus a b & circumscibatur ei quadratum c g: & ipsa c d du pla sit d e : ipsius etiam c d, sit e f pars septima. Quoniam igitur c e ad c d eam habet proportionê,

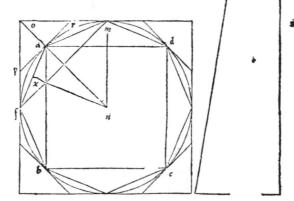

quam uicenum primum ad septenum tenet : i c d uero ad e f etiam, quam septenum

But we must do all this with infinite discretion, because otherwise we shall land ourselves in an imaginary world that bears no relation to the world in which we live.

Hoskin: So that even when you have made up your mind to use mathematics you need great skill and judgement in deciding which properties your mathematical model ought to have.

Galileo: Yes, and this was where Archimedes was so brilliant. For example, when he discussed the laws of the balance his weights always hung by strings that were precisely parallel, even though he knew that their directions really met at the centre of the world. You see, the difference was negligible, and to try to take it into account from the start would have made things impossibly complicated, and quite pointlessly so. In the same way, his floating bodies will have perfect mathematical shapes, whereas the branch of a tree has bumps and rough edges and the water these bodies float in has no colour or taste or smell. There are no fishes swimming in it or logs floating in it. The only properties the water has are mathematical ones. And yet theorems about paraboloids floating in this mathematical water help us to understand how a branch lies in the water of the stream.

Hoskin: And I suppose an experiment is in some sense a bridge between the real world and the ideal world of mathematics. It takes place in the real world, but under such strict conditions and with so many of the unnecessary complications excluded, that in a way it's already got one foot in the ideal world.

Galileo: In my book I describe my experiences with a ball rolling on an inclined plane. I emphasise that the groove has to be very straight and smooth and polished and lined with very smooth parchment, and that the bronze ball must be hard and smooth and very round.

Hoskin: Much closer to a perfect mathematical sphere than, say, a pebble you might pick up on the beach.

Galileo: Yes. I described it all in my book.

Hoskin: Described? And you did say earlier 'my account'. But isn't the book written in the form of a discussion between three friends?

Galileo: Yes, between Sagredo, who is a sensible chap ready to learn the right things, and Simplicio . . .

Hoskin: . . . who, as his name implies, is the spokesman for Aristotle . . .

Galileo: . . . and Salviati, who speaks for me. It is Salviati who describes the experiences – in answer to a request from Simplicio!

Hoskin: So it is the Aristotelian who asks for experiments, and not Salviati.

Galileo: Yes – you remember I told you earlier of another occasion when the Aristotelians challenged me to produce experiments for them.

Hoskin: And the experiments Salviati describes come as close as possible to mathematical perfection.

Galileo: Yes. But there were some things poor old Salviati could not do. For example, the mathematical balls I postulated moved in a vacuum, but a real experimental ball rolls in the air.

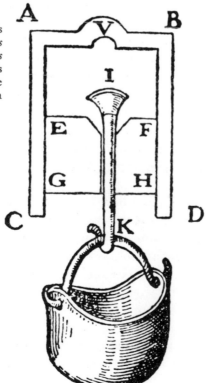

A figure from Galileo's greatest work, *Discourses on Two New Sciences* (1638), illustrating his discussion of the force exerted by a vacuum

Hoskin: But you say in your book that you did the experiments hundreds of times and always got the results exactly right – to within as little as a tenth of a pulsebeat – every single time!

Galileo (laughing): Well, yes, but don't forget that it is Salviati who reports the accuracy of the experiments, not I.

Hoskin (seriously): This sounds to me like a deliberate attempt to mislead the reader.

Galileo: No, no, that stage in the book's argument was no place to embark on a discussion of experimental error. All that mattered was that the experiments should give the results expected, near enough.

Hoskin: So you knew what to expect?

Galileo: Oh yes. You see, I was convinced that nature speaks the language of mathematics, so when I asked myself how a body falls freely I knew the answer must be a mathematical formula. The question was, which one? Now think of the way a fish swims, or a bird flies. Could anything happen more easily, more simply! But surely free fall is the simplest of all natural movements . . .

Hoskin: . . . and so must be represented by the simplest formula.

Galileo: Just so. Now the question was to decide which is the simplest formula. There seemed to me to be two candidates. The speed of the falling body could increase uniformly either with the time, or with the distance.

It took me some time to sort these two out, but finally I discovered that the second one is *logically* impossible, and so I knew that the speed must increase with the time.

Hoskin: And so this is how Galileo would have us believe he discovered that the speed of a freely-falling body increases directly with the time! But Galileo made a mistake. He thought he could prove that speed increasing with distance is *logically* impossible. But surely that's not so. If a man is one mile from a town and walking at one mile per hour, there is nothing logically impossible about his gradually increasing speed until when he is two miles from the town he is walking at two miles per hour. Of course he might find it difficult to get started at all under this formula, but that's a different story.

In his book Galileo goes on to tell us the steps of the argument that led to the experiments with a ball rolling down an inclined plane, and it is once again nine parts inspiration and one part confusion. His law of free fall connects time and speed; but he can't measure speed – there were no speedometers in those days and the very concept of speed was a novelty – so he does some mathematics and changes the formula into one connecting time and distance. But he hasn't a stopwatch so he can't measure very short time intervals! What he does is to look on free fall as a special case of fall down an inclined plane where the whole movement is slowed to the point where he can hope to use his waterclock.

Now this step isn't quite right – because in rolling down a plane a ball not only moves forward more quickly but it also turns more quickly, and this doesn't happen in free fall. But it gets Galileo to the stage where where he can at least *talk* about testing the law by experiments.

Signor, all this seems a lot of hard work for very little.

Galileo: Ah, but as I said earlier, I had added something definite to our knowledge of moving bodies; and I like to think I had shown just how problems like this should be tackled. Besides, I was able to prove dozens more theorems just by mathematics alone, without any further need of experiments.

Hoskin: For example?

Galileo: For example, I showed that a cannon ball in a vacuum will move in a parabolic path.

The diagram is in the book. It shows how in the vertical direction the cannon ball is simply falling straight down, and as we saw just now I knew all about that kind of movement. Horizontally the cannon ball moves with constant speed.

Hoskin: I must ask you about that in a moment.

Galileo: And so all I had to do was to combine these two movements mathematically and show that the path you get is a parabola.

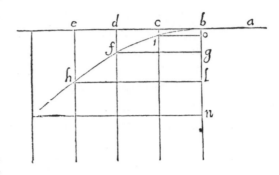

Galileo's diagram illustrating his argument that a projectile (in a non-resisting medium) follows a parabolic path. Horizontally the body moves with uniform speed, covering equal distances *bc*, *cd*, *de*, . . . in successive units of time. Vertically the body accelerates in accordance with Galileo's law of free fall, covering increasing distances *og*, *gl*, *ln*, . . . Galileo assumes these two motions can simply be combined mathematically to produce the path of the projectile, and he shows that this path is a parabola. From *Discourses on Two New Sciences*

Hoskin: Very nice!

Galileo: Of course, an Aristotelian would be uneasy about simply combining two different motions mathematically.

Hoskin: I suppose this would be because he would think of movements in terms of purposes, and two different purposes might clash.

Galileo: Yes; but I had shown that *all* bodies fall in the same way, *whatever* their nature. In other words, we can discuss the mathematics of *how* they fall without worrying about what they *are* or what perfection they are capable of.

Hoskin: You said a cannon ball moves horizontally with constant speed?

Galileo: Yes.

Hoskin: In a straight line?

Galileo: No, horizontally, following the horizon: it is motion *about* the centre of the Earth that is constant – in other words, circular motion.

Hoskin: Could you explain this?

Galileo: You see, if we have a body moving down a smooth slope, then it gathers speed as it goes. If we give it a push up a smooth slope, then it slows down. We all know this from experience. So what happens to a body on a smooth

horizontal surface? The surface does not slope down-
ward – so why should the body gather speed; it doesn't
slope upwards, so why should the body slow down.

Hoskin: In other words, it will keep going at the same speed.

Galileo: Yes, for as long as the surface lasts.

Hoskin: Round and round the Earth, if the surface of the Earth
were perfectly smooth and flat.

Galileo: Precisely.

Hoskin: And this is motion in a circle, not in a straight line.

Galileo: Yes.

Hoskin: But this must make the mathematics of your cannon-ball
very awkward?

Galileo: Ah, well, here we can regard the horizontal motion as in
a straight line, because the range of a cannon is so small
compared to the size of the Earth. We must take advantage of the fact that the difference is negligible, as
Archimedes taught us to do.

Hoskin: I suppose the really significant point is that the horizontal
motion is permanent – something an Aristotelian could
never accept because for him this permanent motion
would serve no purpose.

Galileo: Yes, and it is because this motion is permanent that we
are unaware of it. This is *why* we are unaware that the
Earth is moving and ourselves with it.

And at first sight the Aristotelian argument seems so
conclusive!

Hoskin: What argument is that?

Galileo: Well, it took many forms. Aristotle himself put it this
way. Let's suppose, he would argue, that the Earth is
moving. Right then: Have an archer shoot an arrow up
into the air. Now that arrow takes some time to reach
the ground again – long enough for the Earth, and the
archer with it, to have moved quite a way.

Hoskin: In other words, the arrow would hit the Earth some considerable distance from the archer.

Galileo: That's right. But in fact it falls dangerously near the
archer – and this seems to prove that the Earth is not
moving after all.

Hoskin: I've heard another variation on that. Imagine a butler trying to pour some wine. Now, that wine-glass is dash-ing along with the Earth, so the butler will need to take a compass bearing and find out which way the glass is moving before he lets the wine out of the bottle! But in fact we all know that pouring wine is not all that diffi-cult . . .

Galileo: . . . in the early part of the evening.

Hoskin: So the Earth can't be moving after all!

Galileo: Very good. I like to think in terms of a man dropping a stone from the top of a tower. The Aristotelians would say that because the stone falls at the foot of the tower this proves that the tower hasn't moved and therefore the Earth hasn't moved.

Hoskin: A nice example of a crucial experiment. It seems to settle the question once and for all.

Galileo: But only within the framework of the Aristotelian ideas of movement. They teach that if I let a stone go, then the stone sets off towards the centre of the Earth – because that is the place to which heavy bodies belong in the scheme of things. This kind of motion they call 'natural'. But if I throw the stone upwards, so that it is forced further away from its proper place, then this is 'forced' motion and an external agent must be at work – in this case, my hand. And they see no reason why a stone dropped from a tower and setting off for the centre of the Earth should at the same time chase after the tower –

Hoskin: You mean, if the tower and the whole of the Earth is moving?

Galileo: Yes – so as still to be alongside the tower when it finally hits the ground.

Hoskin: And what you had to do was to create a *new* philosophy in which the stone-dropping experiment settled nothing.

Galileo: Yes.

Hoskin: How did you do this?

Galileo: Well, it's a long story. It began with my focusing atten-tion on horizontal motion – this puts the Aristotelians in a quandary for they find it hard to know whether to call this 'natural' or 'violent'! – and it involved thinking hard about stones falling from towers and other stones falling *from the masts of moving ships, and whether a javelin dropped from a galloping horse may move in the same way as one thrown from a motionless horse.*

Hoskin: You mean that in each case the *hand* of the thrower is moving forward and that's all that matters to the javelin?

Galileo: Yes, and so a javelin dropped from a galloping horse is at that moment being propelled forward by the hand of the rider; and therefore as it falls to the ground it will continue to move forward and keep pace with the horse.

Hoskin: And it will hit the ground alongside the horse, whatever the speed of the horse?

Galileo: Yes, the rider sees the javelin fall beside him, just as it does when the horse is standing still.

Hoskin: And so dropping a javelin is no way to find out if your horse is moving.

Galileo: Neither is dropping a stone from a tower any way to find out if the tower and the Earth are moving.

Hoskin: All this involved thinking hard, rather than actually carrying out experiments. But didn't your observations with the telescope help to establish the Copernican theory of the motion of the Earth round the Sun?

Galileo: My spyglass didn't meet the real need, which was to explain away these stone-dropping experiments . . .

One of many figures in Galileo's *Starry Messenger* (1610) to illustrate his claim that Jupiter has four satellites or moons which orbit about the planet. The existence of a centre of motion in the universe other than the Earth was incompatible with Aristotelian philosophy. Galileo's work also answered an objection against the Copernican position, for previously the Copernicans had appeared to assign to the Earth a unique status as the only planet to possess a satellite

rectam conftituebant; media enim occidétalium pau-
lulum à recta Septentrionem verfus deflectebat. Abe-
rat orientalior à Ioue minuta duo: reliquarum, &
Iouis intercapedines erant fingulæ vnius tantum mi-
nuti. Stellæ omnes eandem præ fe ferebant magnitu-
dinem; ac licet exiguam, lucidiffimæ tamen erant, ac
fixis eiufdem magnitudinis longe fplendidiores.

Die decimaquarta nubilofa fuit tempeftas.

Die decimaquinta, hora noctis tertia in proximè
depicta fuerunt habitudine quatuor Stellæ ad Iouem;

Ori.　　　◯　　✴ ✴ ✳　　✳　　　**Occ.**

occidentales omnes: ac in eadem proxim recta linea
difpofitæ; quæ enim tertia à Ioue numerabatur pau-
lulum

Hoskin: Which, after all, were borne out by our common-sense impressions of the Earth being at rest . . .

Galileo: Yes; but on the other hand there are many intelligent people who find it easier to accept things they can see with their own eyes rather than listen to a lot of talk about natural and violent motion. But some prejudiced professors wouldn't even look! They simply refused to look through my spyglass.

Still, to be fair, I must admit that curved glass has always been the traditional way to create illusions – you know, at fairs and that sort of thing. So the idea that two bits of curved glass could tell them the truth about heaven and earth took a bit of swallowing.

I was cross at the time, though. So I told the poor creatures who earned their living by quoting Aristotle that my spyglass meant that everything written up to now was superseded, and that made me feel better.

Hoskin: I suppose that up to the moment when the telescope was invented each generation had had access to essentially the same facts of nature as its predecessors.

Galileo: Yes, if we leave aside voyages to new lands and things of that sort.

Hoskin: But now you had an advantage over the ancients. You had seen things of which they had never even dreamt!

Galileo: Yes. I had seen mountains on the Moon, spots on the Sun, four small planets going round Jupiter.

Hoskin: But one thing you couldn't see was the Earth going round the Sun. All you could see, surely, were the Earth, Sun, Venus and the rest moving *relatively* to each other. The appearances would be the same whichever was in fact at rest.

Galileo: True, though anything that threw the Aristotelians on the defensive was of some help.

Hoskin: Like these spotty imperfections on the Sun!

Galileo: Yes. But what you said just now needs qualification. According to Ptolemy the Earth is at the centre of the world and the planet Venus always lies more or less between us and the Sun. This means that if Venus shines by the reflected light of the Sun, then the bright side

Galileo

Galileo in old age, from the portrait by Justus Sustermans, c. 1636, in the Uffizzi Gallery

A large astrolabe in a table mounting, believed to have been owned and used by Galileo. (*Museo di Storia della Scienza di Firenze*)

Tycho Brahe (1546-1601) and his great mural quadrant. The King of Denmark helped Tycho to construct on the Baltic island of Hveen a magnificent observatory called Uraniborg, and there for more than twenty years Tycho used instruments of enormous size to make astronomical observations which in accuracy approached the limits possible in the era before the telescope. In the background we see other scenes of work at the observatory. From *Astronomiae Instauratae Mechanica* (Hveen, 1598)

Two of Galileo's telescopes and, in the centre of the ornate frame, one of his object lenses. (*Museo di Storia della Scienza di Firenze*)

An early Italian compound microscope attributed to Galileo (but possibly of later date). (*Museo di Storia della Scienza di Firenze*)

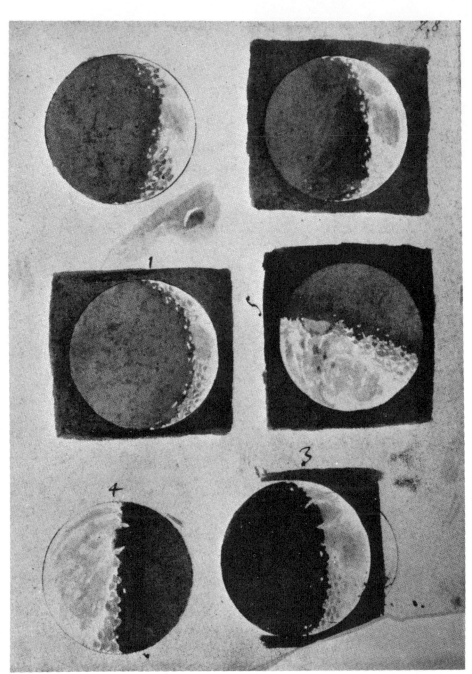

Sketches by Galileo of telescopic observations of the Moon. Aristotelian doctrine taught that the heavens are perfect in contrast to the imperfect Earth, from which it followed that the Earth could not be a heavenly planet moving about the Sun as Copernicus had claimed. From 1609 Galileo used the telescope to bring new evidence against Aristotle, claiming for example that the heavenly Moon has mountains *just like* the Earth. (*Biblioteca Nazionale Centrale di Firenze*)

Frontispiece of Galileo's *Dialogue on the Two Great World Systems* (1632), the book which led to his condemnation. The men depicted in conversation are not the three characters in the *Dialogue*, but Aristotle, Ptolemy and Copernicus

Sketches by Galileo of changes in sunspots in 1612. This use of the telescope to extend the range of the human eye and so to produce new evidence was gravely embarassing to traditional philosophies, and Galileo was quick to press home his advantage in skilful polemical writings. (*Biblioteca Nazionale Centrale di Firenze*)

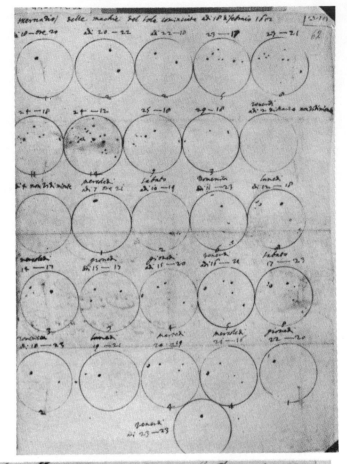

Part of a letter from Galileo, 8 November 1610, in which he discusses mountains on the Moon. (*Biblioteca Nazionale di Firenze*)

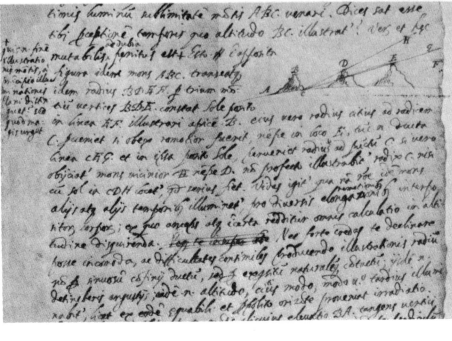

of Venus will always be partly turned away from us.

Hoskin: In other words, we would never see Venus lighted all over like the Moon when it is full.

Galileo: That's right. But I found that Venus in fact goes through phases just like the Moon, and therefore Ptolemy is proved wrong beyond any shadow of doubt.

Hoskin: But just because Ptolemy is wrong this doesn't prove Copernicus is right.

Galileo: Well, for practical purposes we have only a choice between these two.

Hoskin: But what about Tycho Brahe? Didn't he devise a system in which the *relative* motions were much the same as with Copernicus but where it is the Earth that is absolutely at rest. And since your telescope can only see relative motions, it can't possibly rule out Tycho in favour of Copernicus.

Galileo: All Tycho did was to reject the theories of Ptolemy and Copernicus and to promise us a third – and then he failed to carry out his promise! No, the choice must be between Ptolemy and Copernicus, and my spyglass rules out Ptolemy.

Hoskin: And this is why you called your book the *Two Great World Systems.*

Galileo: I was going to call it 'Dialogue on the Tides', because the tides give us physical proof of the Earth's motion, but his Holiness forbade it.

Hoskin: I think perhaps his Holiness did you a service by pushing this alleged proof into the background.

Galileo: If so, then it's the only service he who was once my friend has done me for many a long day. I whose one wish was to serve Holy Mother Church find myself persecuted by her. And I can hope for no relief, because I have committed no crime; if I had done wrong, I could ask for pardon, but because I have been wrongfully sentenced they feel they have to put on a show of strictness.

Of course the Holy Bible can never speak untruth, but God is no less excellently revealed in Nature's action than in the sacred statements of Scripture. I cannot think that the God who has given us senses, and intelligence to use them, meant us to turn our backs on the knowledge they can give us.

Hoskin: Of course there are many things Galileo did in science that I haven't had time to ask him about. For example, his spyglass was not the only way in which he extended the range of the human senses: he played his part in the invention of the thermometer, and of the compound microscope.

But our conversation brought out two points. First, that Galileo did a great deal of very hard thinking; as he said, no one could get very far just by dropping weights from a Leaning Tower. Experiments are questions put to Nature, and we must decide in advance what language we shall use, what questions we shall put and, let's face it, what we think the answers will be. Secondly, Galileo didn't just *argue* that it is possible (and useful) to put questions that involve mathematics, measurement; he *proved* it, by giving us an example, the law of free fall, and all the theorems he showed follow from this law.

And even in science, deeds speak louder than words.

Newton: *The system of the world*

By the middle of the seventeenth century the physical sciences had made rapid strides, but they were still fragmentary and disorganised. Yet there was no shortage of exciting ideas, and the extraordinary power resulting from the combination of mathematics, experiment, and the new apparatus and instruments was widely recognised. What was needed was a mind that could transcend all these partial insights and weld them into a coherent and lasting whole.

Isaac Newton was born in Lincolnshire on Christmas Day, 1642. His father, who had died three months before, had been a yeoman farmer, and Newton as a young man was to have none of the social advantages of many of his contemporaries in the newly-founded Royal Society. He was usually awkward in dealing with his fellow men, and his scientific work was the outcome of solitary labours. Once he was launched on a problem, perhaps by the arrival of a letter or from reading a book, he would keep going under his own steam without feeling the need to share his ideas with colleagues. Fortunately, his characteristic method of working involved drafting and redrafting: it is clear from the mountain of surviving manuscripts that Newton must have spent much of his waking time pen in hand, and little was thrown away. As a result we have a rare opportunity of following the development of one of the most powerful intellects of all time.

At school he was undistinguished, and even after he entered Trinity College, Cambridge, in 1661 his immense powers lay dormant for three more years. But in 1664 he found himself with greater leisure, and he began to read modern scientific works of the first importance, including those of Kepler and Descartes. For much of the following two years the colleges were closed because of the great plague, and by the time the plague was ended

Newton had made epoch-making discoveries in three major fields: in mathematics he had taken major steps in the development of the calculus; in optics he had found that white light is not simple but compound, being made up of different colours; and in dynamics he had begun to tackle the complex problems posed by the observed movements of the Moon and the planets.

Little enough of this was allowed to become public, but Newton was soon elected to a college Fellowship and in 1669 he became Professor of Mathematics. Much of his time he devoted to mathematics and to optics, where his efforts at publication involved him in unwelcome controversy. But for periods he became preoccupied with chemical experiment. At other times he would immerse himself in theology.

His studies of light were eventually published in his *Opticks* which appeared in 1704, after the death of Robert Hooke with whom he had quarrelled bitterly. This book, based on frequent experiments and written in English with the minimum of mathematics and many speculations to guide future research, shows one side to his genius. But the austere *Principia* (1687), in Latin and embedded in immensely difficult mathematics, shows talents of quite a different kind of order. It grew out of the dynamical studies of the plague years, but at that time there had been many reasons why he could not bring this work to a finished conclusion. In particular, he lacked the necessary mathematics, and he did not know enough of Kepler's laws. Accordingly, he put the matter on one side, and as time passed so other mathematicians began to piece together the jigsaw puzzle. Hooke, in particular, had the right basic ideas. This led to quarrels over priority, and it was only by the exercise of exquisite tact on the part of Edmond Halley that Newton was persuaded to give his work to the world in an extended and integrated whole. Poor Halley even had to finance the publication out of his own pocket!

It was worth it! The *Principia* was a vast creation that marked the coming-of-age of the new science. It brought order out of chaos: for example, Newton showed that Kepler's three laws of planetary motion were all consequences of a single law according to which every body in the universe attracts every other body in a definite manner; and that this same law explained the orbits of comets, the movement of the tides, the wobble of the Earth's axis which we know as the precession of the equinoxes, and much, much else besides. And although few readers have ever mastered its contents in detail, it provided the inspiration for studies in mechanics for generations to come.

But Newton was losing his enthusiasm for Cambridge and for natural science. For a while he became Member of Parliament for the University; a little later he fell mentally ill. At last, in 1696, he was appointed Warden of the Mint in London, and three years later became Master. From time to time he showed flashes of his old powers, but in the main he filled the role of Grand Old Man of British science, resting on well-earned laurels. In 1705 he was knighted. For the last quarter-century of his life he was President of the Royal Society. And when he died in 1727, the Lord High Chancellor, two dukes and three earls carried him to his grave in Westminster Abbey. Science had taken its place in national life.

In Newton we meet one of the great geniuses of all time: an austere, remote, intensely powerful mind, capable of immense feats of sustained concentration. He is isolated from his fellow men, although in recent years honour and recognition have come to him in measure so full that even he has mellowed a little. He is held in veneration by his contemporaries, a superman. But he smiles seldom, and has no experience of love or affection. He has been a bachelor all his life, without a single close friend. In earlier years it was difficult to approach him without offence, and the feelers he occasionally extended towards the outside world were unfortunately received and led to an even greater isolation. He still looks on the world with a wary suspicion; and although he has not stretched his mind for years, he still retains his unique power of intellect. He is particularly suspicious of the interviewer, and so is inclined to be haughty and difficult: to give offence to him is all too easy.

Hoskin: 'Nature and Nature's laws lay hid in night, God said, "Let Newton be," and all was light.' This famous epitaph of Alexander Pope gives an eighteenth-century layman's view of Newton's achievement. In the words of someone better able to judge, the French mathematician Lagrange, 'He was the greatest genius who ever lived, and the most fortunate: because only once can someone find a system of the world to establish.'

Of course, we who live after Einstein take a less simple view of the knowledge that science can give us of the world; but nothing can change the fact that with Newton physical science came of age.

At the time when Newton was an undergraduate in Cambridge Galileo had already demonstrated the power of the mathematical view of the world, and men were very conscious of the importance of observations in science; but they were less clear about the use of experiments as check to theory, and, because they were obsessed with a morbid fear of falling into error, they would often content themselves with simply gathering facts.

The situation was confused but full of possibilities; and it's interesting that in the very age when science was first seen as an enterprise calling for the co-operation of many brains and hands, the man who brought order out of this confusion suffered from psychological handicaps that made friendship with him well-nigh impossible.

Sir Isaac, you have been Master of the Mint ever since 1699.

Newton: Yes.

Hoskin: And for three years before that you were Warden of the Mint.

Newton: Yes, during the great recoinage.

Hoskin: And since 1703 you have been President of the Royal Society.

Newton: Yes.

Hoskin: This life as a prominent public figure must contrast strongly with your thirty-odd years in a Cambridge College.

Newton: Thirty-five years – I entered Trinity College in 1661. But even in Cambridge I was not free from meddlesome correspondence in my later years, and I was twice a Member of Parliament.

Hoskin: Let's see, how old were you in 1661?

Newton: Eighteen – I was born on Christmas Day, 1642. My mother told me that I was so small that I might have been put into a quart mug; and two women sent to fetch medicine for me did not expect to find me alive on their return.

Hoskin: Your father was a farmer, wasn't he?

Newton: Yes. He had died just before I was born.

Hoskin: So your mother sent you to a grammar school until you were ready to go to Cambridge!

Newton: Except for some months when she recalled me to help her manage her farm.

Hoskin: What subjects did you have to study in Cambridge?

Newton: I read such works as Aristotle's *Ethics* and logic, with many commentaries . . .

Hoskin: I imagine the courses were not very different from what they had been in medieval times.

Newton: No. It was not until 1664 that I read the *Geometry* of

An example of Newton's method of study in the middle 1660s. Top: Upper and lower bounds for the value of $\frac{4}{\pi}$ (denoted by ☐), from John Wallis's *Arithmetica Infinitorum* (1655). Below: Newton's notes on Wallis's argument (in which $\frac{4}{\pi}$ is now denoted by a), written in the winter of 1664/65. (*Cambridge University Library Add MS 4000, 17*[r])

Et (continuata ejuſmodi operatione juxta Tabellæ leges) invenietur

$$\square \begin{cases} \text{minor quam } \dfrac{3 * 3 \times 5 \times 5 \cdot 7 \times 7 * 9 \times 9 * 11 \times 11 \times 13 \times 13}{2 \times 4 \times 4 \times 6 \times 6 \times 8 \times 8 \times 10 * 10 * 12 * 12 \times 14} \times \sqrt{1\,\tfrac{1}{14}}. \\[2mm] \text{major quam } \dfrac{3 \times 3 \times 5 \times 5 * 7 \times 7 \times 9 \times 9 \times 11 \times 11 \times 13 \times 13}{2 \times 4 \times 4 \times 6 \times 6 \times 8 * 8 \times 10 \times 10 \times 12 \times 12 \times 14} \times \sqrt{1\,\tfrac{1}{14}}. \end{cases}$$

Et ſic deinceps quouſq; libet. Ita nempe ut fractionis Numerator fiat continue multiplicando numeros impares 3, 5, 7, &c. bis poſitos; Denominator vero, continue multiplicando numeros pares, 2, 4, 6, &c, bis item poſitos, exceptis primo & ultimo, qui ſemel ponuntur : Et tota deniq; ratio ſeu fractio, ſic facta, ducatur in Radicem-quadraticam Unitatis aliquotâparte ſuî auctæ; eâ nempe quæ denominatorem habet eum qui eſt ultimus numerorum, continue multiplicatorum, imparium, ſi quæramus numerum juſto majorem, vel parium, ſi juſto minorem.

Atq; hoc pacto eouſq; tandem pervenietur donec majoris & minoris differentia evadat quavis aſſignata minor; (quæ propterea, ſi ſupponatur in infinitum continuanda operatio, tandem

B b b 2   dem

Descartes, and the works of Wallis, and Oughtred's *Clavis* . . .

Hoskin: These are all mathematical texts?

Newton: Yes. It was at this time that I found the method of infinite series. And in the summer of 1665, being forced from Cambridge by the plague, I computed the area under the hyperbola to fifty-two figures.

Hoskin: Quite a computing marathon!

Newton: The same year in May I found the method of tangents, and in November I had the direct method of fluxions . . .

Hoskin (*vainly trying to break in*): That means . . .

Newton: And the next year in January I had the theory of colours; and in May following I had entrance into the inverse method of fluxions. And the same year I began to think of gravity extending to the Moon, and I deduced the forces which keep the planets in their orbits . . .

Hoskin (*finally breaking in*): Could I interrupt you for a moment please, before we get lost. I must say this shows a truly fantastic burst of energy on your part – and this was all done at a time when the normal studies were interrupted by an outbreak of plague.

Newton: Yes, all this was in the two plague years 1665 and 1666 . . .

Hoskin: When you were twenty-two or twenty-three. It almost looks as though the plague gave you a chance to work in peace at last.

Newton: I was in the prime of my age for invention, and minded mathematics and philosophy more than any time since.

Hoskin: . . . meaning by 'philosophy' '*natural* philosophy' – what we would call experimental science.

Now, could we go back for a moment? You talked about three areas in which you worked at this time: you first of all mentioned infinite series and tangents and fluxions – this is all to do with that branch of mathematics we call the calculus. Then you spoke of your theory of colours.

Newton: Yes.

Hoskin: And finally you were telling us about gravity extending to the Moon and the forces which control the movements of the planets?

Newton: Yes.

Hoskin: Could I ask about each of these in turn? On the matter of the calculus, I believe that the notation dx and dy, and so on, which mathematicians use today and which is taught in schools, comes from your German contemporary, Leibniz. Does this mean that Leibniz was the first to invent the calculus?

Newton: Quite the contrary, although he and his friends did all in their power to take the honour from me. In the end the Royal Society appointed a committee to look into the matter. 'The methods of Mr Leibniz and Mr Newton,' they said, 'are the same, excepting the name and mode of notation. We therefore take the proper question to be, Who was the first inventor of the method? and we believe that those who have reputed Mr Leibniz the first inventor knew little or nothing of Mr Newton's having that method above fifteen years before Mr Leibniz began to publish it. For which and other reasons we reckon Mr Newton the first inventor.'

Hoskin: You can quote this so well from memory one might almost think you had written it yourself . . .

Newton: What if I did!

Hoskin: . . . and in any case you were President of the Royal Society, and one of your own committees could hardly be expected to be impartial.

Newton: Sir, the committee was numerous and skilful and composed of gentlemen of several nations.

Hoskin: But if you had a fifteen year lead on Leibniz, why did you allow him to get into print first?

Newton: Sir, I tried, but found our booksellers would publish nothing weighty that was mathematical.

Hoskin: Because, presumably, they had lost so much money in the Great Fire of London.

Newton: Yes, but in any case when I first published my theory of colours I found such a stir raised against me that I made myself a slave in settling disputes. And I determined resolutely to bid adieu to philosophy eternally, excepting what I might do for my private satisfaction or leave to come out after me.

Hoskin: You mean, you made up your mind not to publish anything more?

Newton: Yes. I saw a man must either resolve to put out nothing new, or become a slave to defend it.

Hoskin: Well, history of science would be the poorer if you had continued in this mood all your life. But how did this dispute about colours come about?

Newton: When I was elected a fellow of the Royal Society in 1672 . . .

Hoskin: Excuse me, the Royal Society was founded in 1660, wasn't it?

Newton: Yes.

Hoskin: And many of the members who took part in the weekly experiments and discussions were amateurs in science. In fact you were one of the few professionals.

Newton: When I joined I was Professor of Mathematics in Cambridge.

Hoskin: Did you ever try to start similar meetings in Cambridge?

Newton: Yes, but that which chiefly dashed the business was the want of persons willing to try experiments.

Hoskin: Anyway, you were saying, when you became a Fellow of the Royal Society . . .

Newton: . . . I desired to show my duty to them by communicating an account of a discovery which was in my judgement the oddest, if not the most considerable, detection which had hitherto been made in the operations of nature.

Hoskin: And this was your theory of colours – which dated from the time of the plague.

Newton: Yes. In the beginning of the year 1666 I procured me a triangular glass prism. And having darkened my chamber, and made a small hole in my window-shuts, to let in a convenient quantity of the Sun's light, I placed my prism at its entrance.

Hoskin: So that the spectrum would fall on the opposite wall.

Newton: Yes. It was at first a very pleasing divertisement to view the vivid and intense colours produced thereby; but after a while, applying myself to consider them more carefully, I became surprised to see them in an oblong form.

Hoskin: What shape would you have expected the spectrum to have?

Newton: I expected it to be circular from the position in which I had placed my prism. When I found it was not, I examined every possible explanation for this, and I made many experiments. Eventually I concluded that light is not simple but consists of distinct rays, some of which are more refrangible than others.

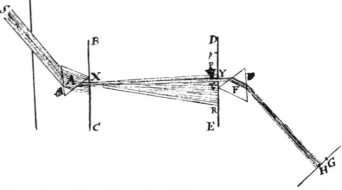

Newton's crucial experiment from his first paper on colours, sent to the Secretary of the Royal Society in 1672. Light from the Sun S passes through a prism A, and as A is rotated different colours pass through the (fixed) slits X and Y and the fixed prism F before striking the far wall. Newton found that the different colours (qualities) were associated with different positions G, H (quantities). (From a revised diagram intended for an abortive printing in 1677 of Newton's early optical correspondence, *Cambridge University Library Add MS 4002, 128a*)

Hoskin: I see. Other people thought that white light was simple, and that one changed the qualities of white light to give it colour.

Newton: Yes.

Hoskin: But you showed that white light is compound – that it is made up of a mixture of colours, and each was bent through a different angle.

Newton: Exactly. And to the same degree of refrangibility ever belongs the same colour; and to the same colour ever belongs the same degree of refrangibility.

Hoskin: You mean that you can label each ray of light according *either* to its colour *or* to the angle through which it is bent by passing through a given prism.

Newton: Yes.

Hoskin: In other words, we can study light in terms of these

Newton

Newton in old age, by John
Vanderbank, 1725, in the
National Portrait Gallery

Part of Trinity College,
Cambridge, from *Cantabrigia
Illustrata* by David Loggan. The
rooms on the first floor between
the chapel and Great Gate are
those occupied by Newton in
the 1680s, when he composed
the *Principia*. The garden in
front is Newton's and the small
lean-to shed against the chapel
wall in the corner of the garden
is where he made numerous
chemical experiments

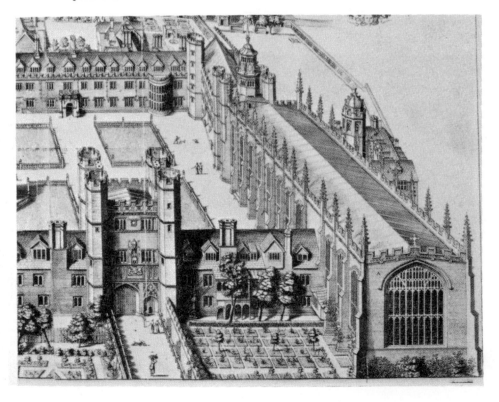

Manuscript in Newton's hand in which he explains the fluxional anagram he communicated to Leibniz in October 1676, for the 'report' of the committee set up by the Royal Society to decide the priority dispute between Newton and Leibniz over the invention of the calculus. (*Cambridge University Library Add MS 3977 §8.1ʳ*)

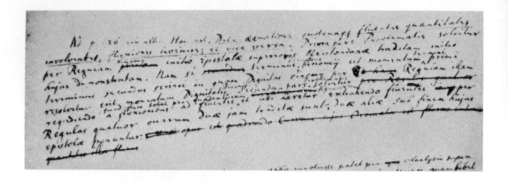

Comments on Newton's theory of colours by the French Jesuit Ignatius Pardies, one of several criticisms published in the *Philosophical Transactions*. Such criticisms were unwelcome to Newton, but the journal performed an important service as an international forum for scientific debate

(4087)

A Latin Letter written to the Publiſher *April* 9. 1672. n. ſt:
by *Ignatius Gaſton Pardies* P. Prof. of the Mathematicks in the Pariſian Colledge of *Clermont* ; containing
ſome Animadverſions upon Mr. *Iſaac Newton*, Prof. of the
Mathematicks in the Univerſity of *Cambridge*, his *Theory of
Light*, printed in N°. 80.

*L**Egi ingenioſiſſimam Hypotheſin de* Lumine & Coloribus
Clariſſimi Newtoni. *Et quia nonnullam Ego operam dedi
in iſta contemplatione atque Experimentis peragendis, perſcribam ad
Te pauca, quæ mihi circa novam iſtam doctrinam occurrerunt.*

*Circa ipſam Luminis naturam illud profectò extraordinarium vide-
tur, quòd ait vir eruditiſſimus, Lumen conſtare ex aggregatione
infinitorum propemodum radiorum. qui ſuâpte indole ſuam quiſque
colorem referant retineantque, atque adeò nati apti ſint certà qua-
dam & peculiari ratione, plus alij, alij minus, refringi : Radios
ejuſmodi, dum promiſcui in aperto lumine confunduntur, nullatenus
diſcerni; ſed candorem potiùs referre ; in refractione verò ſingulos
unius coloris ab aliis alterius coloris ſecerni, & hoc modo ſecretos,
ſub proprio & nativo colore apparere : Ea corpora ſub aliquo colore,
v. g. rubro, videri, quæ apta ſint reflectere aut tranſmittere radios ſolummodò rubros, &c.*

*Iſtæc tam extraordinaria Hypotheſis, quæ, ut ipſe obſervat, Di-
optricæ fundamenta evertit, praxéſque hactenus inſtitutas inutiles
reddit, tota nititur illo Experimento Priſmatis Cryſtallini, ubi radij per foramen fenoſtræ intra obſcurum cubiculum ingreſſi, ac deinde
in parietem impacti, aut in charta recepti, non in rotundum confor-
mati,* ut ipſi, ad regulas refractionum receptas attendenti,
expectandum videbatur, *ſed in oblongam figuram extenſi apparu-
erunt : Unde concluſit, oblongam ejuſmodi figuram ex eo eſſe, quòd
nonnulli radij minus, nonnulli magis refringerentur.*

Sed mihi quidem videtur juxta communes & receptas *Dioptricæ*
leges *figuram illam, non rotundam, ſed oblongam eſſe oportere. Cùm
enim radij ex oppoſitis diſci Solaris partibus procedentes, variam
habeant in ipſo tranſitu Priſmatis inclinationem, variè quoque refringi debent : ut cùm unorum inclinatio* 30 *ſaltem minutis major
ſit inclinatione aliorum, major quoque evadat illorum Refractio.*

Xxxx   *Igitur*

Fundamentum harum Operationum, fatis obvium quidèm, (quoniam jam non poffum Explicationem ejus profequi,) fic potius celavi * $6accdæ$ $13eff7i3l9n4o4qrr4f9t12vx.$

Hoc fundamento conatus fum etiam reddere † fpeculationes de Quadratura Curvarum fimpliciores ; pervenique ad Theoremata quædam generaliora. Et, ut candide agam, ecce primum Theorema.

Ad Curvam aliquam fit $dz^\theta \times \overline{e + fz^n}|^\lambda$ Ordinatim-applicata, termino abfciffæ feu bafis z normaliter infiftens : ubi literæ d, e, f denotant quaflibet quantitates Datas ; & θ, n, λ indices Poteftatum five Dignitatum quantitatum quibus affixæ funt. Fac $\frac{\theta+1}{n} = r$, $\lambda+r=s$, $\frac{d}{nf} \times \overline{e + fz^n}|^{\lambda+1} = Q$, & $rn - n = \varpi$: & Area Curvæ erit Q in $\frac{z^\varpi}{s} - \frac{r-1}{s-1} \times \frac{eA}{fz^n} + \frac{r-2}{s-2} \times \frac{eB}{fz^n}$ $- \frac{r-3}{s-3} \times \frac{eC}{fz^n} + \frac{r-4}{s-4} \times \frac{eD}{fz^n}$ &c. literis A, B, C, D &c. denotantibus terminos proxime antecedentes ; nempe A terminum $\frac{z^\varpi}{s}$, B terminum $- \frac{r-1}{s-1} \times \frac{eA}{fz^n}$ &c. Hæc Series, ubi r fractio eft vel numerus negativus, continuatur in infinitum ; ubi vero r integer eft & affirmativus, continuatur ad tot terminos tantum quot funt Unitates in eodem r ; & fic exhibet Geometricam Quadraturam Curvæ. Rem Exemplis illuftro.

* Hoc eft, *Data Æquatione quotcunque fluentes quantitates involvente, Fluxiones invenire; & vice verfa.* Prior pars Problematis folvitur per Regulam Binomii initio Epiftolæ fuperioris *Newtoniana* traditam & initio hujus demonftratam. Nam fi terminus fecundus Binomii fit momentum termini primi, terminus fecundus Seriei, in quam dignitas Binomii per Regulam illam refolvitur, erit momentum Dignitatis Binomii. Pofterior pars Problematis folvitur regrediendo a momentis ad fluentes : quod ubi hæretur fieri folet quadrando figuras ; & ubi ad quadraturas hæretur, extrahendo fluentes per Regulas quatuor, quarum duas *Newtonus* in Epiftola priore explicuit, duas alias fub finem hujus Epiftolæ literis tranfpofitis occultavit, ut mox dicetur.

† Hujufmodi Theoremata *Newtono* ante annum 1669 innotuiffe patet, per Analyfin fupra impreffam pag. 18, lin. 31, ut & per hanc Epiftolam.

Part of the printed report,
Commercium Epistolicum (1712/13),
anonymously edited 'for the
Royal Society'.
Compare Newton's draft
with the first printed footnote

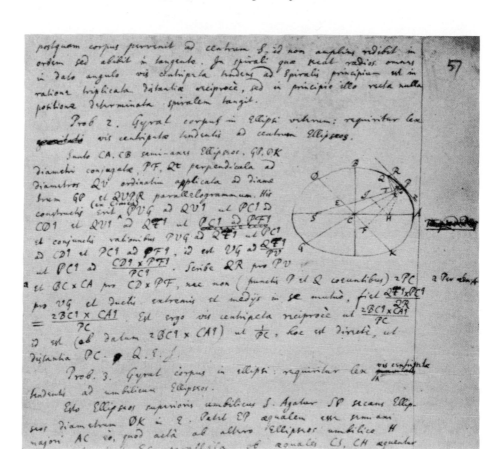

Figure and opening lines of Newton's fundamental proof that elliptical orbits may be traversed under an inverse-square 'gravity' to a focus (*De Motu Corporum*, autumn 1684): similar proofs hold for the parabola and hyperbola. (*Cambridge University Library Add MS* 3965 §7.57ʳ)

Newton's (second) reflecting telescope. Although in itself of limited value, this design pointed the way to a solution of grave problems inherent in refracting telescopes, which in Newton's day were necessarily of excessive length.

angles which we can measure, without having to worry about what colour it looks like to us.

Newton: That is so.

Hoskin: Could you give us an example of another of your experiments.

Newton: One thing I did was to use a lens to bring all the colours of the spectrum together once more.

Hoskin: In other words, your prism broke the white light up into its component parts, and the lens brought them together again and gave you white light once more.

Newton: Yes. If you pass light through the prism and then through the lens, and if you then intercept this light with a sheet of white paper, you will see the colours converted into whiteness again by being mingled.

Hoskin: And this was only one of a number of experiments you gave in support of your hypothesis.

Newton: My design was not to devise an hypothesis; what I did was to enquire diligently into the properties of light, and to establish these properties by experiments. We must afterwards proceed more slowly to hypotheses for the explaining of them. But I chose to decline all hypotheses, and to speak of light in general terms.

Hoskin: Let me see if I understand. You have established by your experiments not what light is, but how light behaves.

Newton: Yes; I derived my theory directly and positively from experiments. This is the way we must discover the properties of things, by deducing them from experiments.

Hoskin: And we can if we wish go on later to consider hypotheses such as, that light consists of little particles moving in ether, or something of that sort; but this is not what you were doing in this early work of yours. Did your readers understand this distinction?

Newton: No. The disputes were intolerable. They claimed I had proposed an hypothesis, and then put forward hypotheses of their own. They would have me explain *their* experiments on *my* hypothesis; and they insisted they had tried my experiments, and denied they succeeded as I had described them.

Was I bound to satisfy them? It seems they thought it

not enough to propound objections unless they might
insult me for my inability to answer them all. But how
did they know that I did not think them too weak to
require an answer? In the end I refused to see any more
letters on the subject.

Hoskin: When did you decide to do that?

Newton: In 1678 – six years after my first paper was published! By
then I had for some time past been endeavouring to bend
myself from philosophy to other studies, so that I grudged
the time spent in philosophy, unless it be perhaps at idle
hours sometimes for a diversion.

Hoskin: But you still had your duties as professor.

Newton: I was to lecture one hour a week each term, and to keep
the door of my room open at times to answer difficulties.

Hoskin: And you say this left plenty of time for your other
studies. What were they?

Newton: I did something on chronology.

Hoskin: What, you mean dates? Battles and kings and that sort of
thing?

Newton: There is much uncertain about chronologies of ancient
Kingdoms. The Greek antiquities are full of poetical
fictions, because the early Greeks wrote nothing in prose.
And as for the chronology of the Latins, that is still more
uncertain, for the old records were burned by the Gauls,
sixty-four years before the death of Alexander the Great.
The Assyrians are in a worse state still . . .

Hoskin: So what have you done about it?

Newton: For one thing I have drawn up a chronological table, so
as to make chronology suit with the course of nature,
with astronomy, with sacred history, and with itself;
together with a full exposition of my reasons. I also give
an exact account of the size and aspect of the Temple of
Solomon.

Hoskin: How successful do you think you have been?

Newton: I do not pretend my dates to be exact to a year: there may
be errors of five to ten years, and sometimes twenty – but
not much above.

Hoskin: What else did you study?

Newton: I studied divinity; and especially have I tried to expound the prophecies of Daniel and St John.

Hoskin: Do you mean that you use them to foretell the future?

Newton: No, the folly of interpreters has been to foretell times and things by prophecy, as if God designed to make them prophets. The design of God was much otherwise. He gave these books not to gratify men's curiosities by enabling them to foreknow things, but that after they were fulfilled they might be interpreted by the event.

But the time is not yet come for understanding them perfectly, because the main revolution predicted in them is not yet come to pass. 'In the days of the voice of the seventh angel, when he shall begin to sound, the mystery of God shall be finished, as he hath declared to his servants the prophets'; and then 'The kingdoms of this world shall become the kingdoms of our Lord and his Christ, and he shall reign for ever'.

Hoskin: Sir Isaac, you have an exceptional knowledge of the Bible, and yet you have never taken holy orders. Isn't it the case that in your day fellows of Trinity could be compelled to take holy orders? So how do you come to

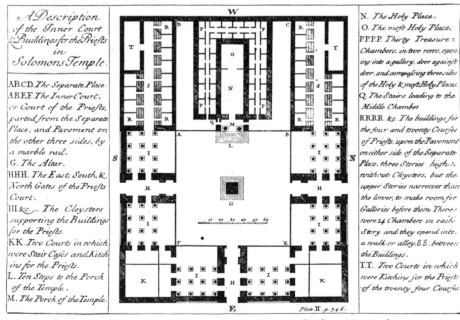

One of the plates illustrating Solomon's Temple, from Newton's
The Chronology of Ancient Kingdoms Amended (1728)

be still a layman?

Newton: As professor, I was granted a dispensation by the King.

Hoskin: But why did you wish to have a dispensation?

Newton: I could serve the Church better as a layman.

Hoskin: Were you perhaps too unorthodox in your views?

Newton: My successor was expelled from the university for proclaiming his disbelief.

Hoskin: Evidently a dangerous topic! All right then. Tell me what else you studied during your years in Cambridge?

Newton: I made chemical experiments to discover the physical qualities of bodies – and my thoughts on the nature of acids have since been published. For about six weeks in the spring and again in the autumn I kept the fire in my laboratory going day and night, my secretary sitting up one night and I the next, until the experiments were finished.

Hoskin: Your secretary tells us about this. He says, 'What his aim might be I was not able to penetrate into, but his pains, his diligence at these set times, made me think he aimed at something beyond the reach of human art and industry.' Does this mean that you were a student of alchemy?

Newton: We must find knowledge where we can. The alchemic authors had great experience in working with fire.

Hoskin: And you followed up the hints they gave about how to make gold.

Newton: My desire was not to profit from multiplying gold.

Hoskin: Maybe not, but you took their claims seriously.

Let me be more definite. For example, did you, on 2 August 1692, soon after the death of Robert Boyle, write to John Locke the philosopher, and explain to him that you did not believe a recipe given him by Boyle would succeed in multiplying gold?

Newton: Peace, peace. Such things are not to be communicated without immense damage to the world, if there should be any truth in the alchemic authors. Let us talk of other matters.

Hoskin: I was being a little unfair to Sir Isaac then, when I implied he was an alchemist, because if the alchemists could have multiplied gold it would have been of the greatest

scientific interest – and also a public disaster. What would
the nation have thought if it had known that the Master
of the Mint was a leading authority on possible methods
of making gold!

We must turn now to the third of the questions
Newton studied during the plague years; and we all know
the story of the apple falling that made him wonder if the
Earth pulls the apple in the same way that it pulls the
Moon and stops it escaping from the Earth. But at this
stage there were many reasons why he could not follow
up these ideas.

For one thing, he did not have the necessary mathematics; and the whole situation was much more confused
than it looks to us in retrospect. Because we live after
Newton, we think of Kepler's laws of planetary motion
as sound, established information on which the mathematicians could work. But the point is that before
Newton showed Kepler's laws followed from his
planetary theory, these laws were based mainly on
observations which, *of course*, were not exact – and
therefore astronomers rightly considered other laws which
fitted the observations just as well. In fact it was many
years before Newton took Kepler's second law seriously.

For the time being he shelved the whole problem; and
meanwhile Robert Hooke (he was in charge of experiments at the Royal Society, and had already opposed
Newton's theory of light) was gradually getting the
essentials of the situation clear – along with Christopher
Wren and Edmond Halley, the astronomer, and others.

They realised that by themselves the planets would
escape from the Sun along the tangents to their orbits,
and that they are continually being pulled back by the
Sun, rather like a stone being whirled on the end of a
string is pulled back by the string. But the stone travels
in a circle, whereas the planets follow a more complicated path, one difficult to handle mathematically.

The problem, in fact, became one of sheer mathematics.

Well, in 1679, Hooke wrote Newton some friendly

letters, raising some of these questions; as usual, Hooke ended by making him angry, but not before he had prodded Newton into examining the motions of the planets once more. This time Newton solved the problem to his satisfaction, and then put it on one side and forgot about it. It wasn't until 1684 that Halley called to ask his help with the mathematics of planetary orbits and was amazed to find that he already knew the answer. With great tact, Halley persuaded Newton to set out his work in full, and in 1687 *The Mathematical Principles of Natural Philosophy*, the *Principia*, was published at Halley's expense.

Newton: But not before Mr Hooke made a great stir at the Royal Society pretending I had it all from him and desiring they would see that he had justice done him!

Hoskin: But it was true to say that he had published most of the essentials of the problem – and all he wanted was a mention in the preface!

Newton: He had done nothing and yet written as if he knew, and had sufficiently hinted, all but what remained to be determined by the drudgery of calculations and observations. He excused himself from that labour by reason of his other business: whereas he should rather have excused himself by reason of his inability.

Now is not this very fine? Mathematicians who find out, settle, and do all the business, must content themselves with being nothing but dry calculators and drudges, and another that does nothing but pretend ...

Hoskin: Sir Isaac, no one wants to take away the great credit that is yours. We all understand that Hooke did no more than throw out some speculations that were in the air. These became established only when you wove your mathematical system around them and then linked them to observations like the motions of the tides and the orbits of the planets. But this wasn't the only controversy your *Principia* gave rise to?

Newton: Mr Leibniz and others called my gravity an occult quality.

Hoskin: I can imagine they were unhappy about the Sun acting on the planets at a distance – and to say that the apple moves towards the Earth 'by gravity' must have sounded to them like the old 'magical sympathies' that used to be dragged in when people couldn't explain something?

Newton: But my theory of gravity is proved by mathematical demonstration, grounded upon experiments and the phenomena of nature. So far, it is true, I have not been able to discover the *cause* of those properties of gravity, and I invent no hypotheses. But it is enough that gravity does really exist, and abundantly serves to account for all the motions of the heavenly bodies and of our sea.

Hoskin: Sir Isaac, when you wrote your *Principia*, did you have any purpose in view outside of science?

Newton: Yes, I had in mind questions that might lead thoughtful men to a belief in God, and nothing rejoices me more than to find it useful for that purpose.

Hoskin: But how does God come into it? Don't your planets just go on and on under the law of gravity?

Newton: Yes, but they could not possibly have derived the regular position of their orbits from such laws.

Hoskin: You're thinking of the way in which Saturn and Jupiter and the rest of the planets all go round the Sun the same way.

Newton: Yes, and the moons of Earth, Jupiter and Saturn turn in *circles* with the *same* direction of motion and nearly in the *same planes* as their planets. It is not to be conceived that mere mechanical causes could give birth to so many regular motions. No, this most beautiful system of the Sun, planets and comets could come only from the counsel and dominion of an intelligent and powerful being. Blind fate could never make all the planets move one and the same way in concentric circles – excepting some minor irregularities which will be apt to increase till the system needs a reformation.

Hoskin: How do you mean?

Newton: The irregularities which may have come from the mutual actions of comets and planets upon one another.

Hoskin: You mean that the comets and planets pull each other and in time this will upset the beautiful pattern which you see in the solar system?

Newton: And the system will then need a reformation.

Hoskin: You mean God has to give the whole thing a push from time to time! Then could I put to you this letter from Mr Leibniz. He writes: 'Sir Isaac Newton and his followers have also a very odd opinion concerning the work of God. According to their doctrine, God Almighty wants to wind up his watch from time to time: otherwise it would cease to move. He had not, it seems, sufficient foresight to make it a perpetual motion. Nay, this machine of God's making is so imperfect that he is obliged to clean it now and then and even to mend it . . . '

Newton: If you read the answer that my friend Dr Samuel Clarke made to Mr Leibniz you will see that he explains that this amendment is only with regard to *our* conceptions. To God the present order *and* the disorder to come *and* the reformation that follows are all *equally* parts of the design framed in God's original perfect idea.

Hoskin: He means that because God planned from the start to intervene from time to time, these interventions are not true miracles.

Newton: Yes.

Hoskin: Sir Isaac, you have spent much of your long life in solitary study. You have no children and few close friends. What do you feel you have accomplished?

Newton: I do not know what I may appear to the world; but to myself I seem to have been only like a boy, playing on the sea-shore and diverting myself in now and then finding a smoother pebble or a prettier shell than ordinary, whilst the great ocean of truth lay all undiscovered before me.

Hoskin: As we have seen, Newton was expert in many fields besides science and mathematics. And even in science, his work in optics was just as influential as his *Principia*, because anyone could read and profit from his *Opticks* whereas the *Principia* is a fearsome task for even a gifted mathematician to read. In fact it's really since the *Principia* that students of nature have been divided into those who can tackle mathematical physics and those who cannot.

But the mathematical argument of the *Principia* must always be his great glory, because it allows him to explain so many of the observed facts of both sky and earth by a single, universal force.

3   Herschel: *The depths of space and time*

Wilhelm Friedrich Herschel, or William Herschel as he was later known, was born in Hanover in 1738, and although his father was only a humble musician, in the Herschel home there was education in the best sense of the word. William Herschel followed in his father's footsteps and studied the violin and oboe, but of an evening the two of them would argue about Newton or Leibniz, or perhaps go out and observe the stars.

In 1757, however, Hanover was occupied by French troops and on his father's advice Herschel fled to England. Fortunately he could turn his hand to every form of musical activity, and it was not long before his unlimited energies were reviving his boyhood interests in studies outside music. He began to read Smith's treatise on *Harmonics*, and from this he progressed to the same author's *Opticks*, with its detailed account of the theory and construction of telescopes, and its outline of the present state of astronomy. Herschel's appetite was whetted. He had by this time been appointed to a secure post as organist of the fashionable Octagon Chapel in Bath, and in 1773 he began to buy astronomical books and instruments. As his musical duties increased, so did his preoccupation with astronomy. The days and nights became more and more crowded, until on 13 March 1781 something happened that was to alter the whole pattern of his life.

That evening, Herschel was at the telescope continuing the systematic survey of the entire sky on which he was currently engaged, when he noticed a 'curious either nebulous star or perhaps a comet'. In fact it proved to be Uranus, the first planet to be discovered since recorded history began. In the long run the discovery was perhaps of no great significance. But it caught the imagination of
61   the world, and Herschel was awarded a Royal Pension

that enabled him to give his full energies to astronomy.

The discovery of Uranus was only one of many contributions Herschel made to our knowledge of the solar system. But his driving passion was for an understanding of the large-scale architecture of the universe, the 'construction of the heavens' as he termed it; and his great achievement was in opening the eyes of astronomers to the wonders that lie beyond our own little corner of the universe.

Now existing telescopes were much too small to detect the fainter and more distant objects. His first job was therefore to build bigger and bigger telescopes, and this meant bigger and bigger mirrors. Herschel soon found that mirrors of the scale he required were not to be bought, and so he had to teach himself how to grind disks into the required shape. His greatest telescope was to have a mirror that weighed a ton and measured four feet across – a large instrument even by modern standards.

Other astronomers had nothing to rival these giant instruments, and Herschel exploited his advantage to the full by sitting out night after night observing whenever moonlight or clouds did not make this impossible. His indomitable courage and resolution transformed what he called the 'natural history' of the heavens, that is, our collections of facts concerning the stars and other more mysterious objects in the sky.

Armed with the best telescopes, and relentless in his observing programmes, Herschel was in a unique position to theorise about the heavens. He alone had access to the facts. Now it often happens in science that those who collect facts have so exaggerated a respect for them that they hesitate to try to transcend them. Not so Herschel. For him it was important to keep a proper balance between fact and theory, and he made no secret of his conviction that it was better to theorise *and speculate* too much rather than too little. In which direction is the solar system travelling? Are there objects beyond the solar system that are not made up of separate bodies like stars and planets? How are stars and star clusters formed?

What is the shape of the Milky Way star system to which our Sun belongs? Are there other Milky Ways in the universe or is ours the only one?

Some of these questions to which Herschel devoted so much effort have now been answered, others are still being explored. In tackling them he pioneered the use of statistical arguments; he conceived of a star system as maturing (or evolving, as we would put it) over enormous periods of time, a process which we short-lived creatures must grasp through the study of *different* systems now at different stages of their development. He even talked of objects so distant that their light had taken millions of years in its journey to us.

But sometimes Herschel's boldness degenerates into recklessness, and then he reveals a less-publicised side of science: the scientist's commitment on non-scientific grounds; his readiness to find in nature what he wants to find; his reluctance to discard an invalidated hypothesis unless he has a substitute for it; and the freedom with which he will make the hypotheses he requires even in the total absence of any evidence in their favour. Herschel died in 1822, tired and old, but in mind he was always a young man in a hurry. As a result he is – perhaps – unusually vulnerable to the questions posterity would like to put to him.

Herschel is now full of years, and has the serenity that comes from a life of monumental achievement. Visitors catch from him a sense of awe at the glory of creation that he has uncovered, where 'millions of years are but moments'. True, he still bears the marks of occasional conflicts with the professional scientists, in which he has once been driven to the verge of a breakdown by his own increasing obstinacy rather than by any improper conduct on the part of his opponents; but otherwise he is at peace. Long ago he set himself great targets which he pursued with unflinching determination, without counting the cost to himself – and unaware of the cost to his nearest and dearest. He has had his share of disappointments, but his achievement has been massive, and he can afford to rest on his laurels. In speech he betrays his German origin and the fact that he did not speak English until his late teens. His manner is calm and courteous, and he is prepared to explain technical matters simply and slowly. Yet one is always conscious of an underlying determination bordering on obstinacy.

Hoskin: In the eighteenth century, astronomy was still centred on the solar system – on the Sun and Moon, planets and comets – as it had been since ancient times. In theory it was known that the stars are other suns, moving in space; but in practice they were still little more than points of light in the sky, a kind of distant backcloth to the motions of the planets. The man who did most to make the stars, and in fact the whole architecture of the universe, part of science was William Herschel.

Herschel was a great pioneer, a man who worked in new fields of study, who asked new questions and thought of new ways of answering them. As a scientist he lived dangerously, and I have always wanted the chance to ask him about what seem to me to be plain contradictions in his theories.

Sir William, when you discovered the planet Uranus in 1781 you were a busy professional musician in middle life. How was it that you came to find the planet? Had you, for example, any idea where to look?

Herschel: On the contrary. No one had ever discovered a new planet since recorded history began, and there was no reason to expect we should find any more.

Hoskin: Then you discovered it by *accident?*

Herschel: Oh no. I was examining the whole sky, piece by piece, and sooner or later the planet's turn was bound to come. You see, I had built myself a telescope good enough to show at a glance that the planet was not a star. In fact at first I thought it must be a comet. But the professional astronomers had difficulty picking it out even when I told them where to look.

Hoskin: And it was *through* this discovery that you became famous?

Herschel: Yes, though not everyone was pleased. When I mentioned my telescopes could magnify six thousand times, people said I was fit to be sent to Bedlam. Still, some friends told me they would be glad to go there with me.

But I learned a lot from that episode. I had had little or no contact with the professional astronomers, and so it never occurred to me that my telescopes were so out of the ordinary. In fact, in the end I had to take one of them down to Greenwich to the Royal Observatory, and set it up alongside theirs. Then they had to admit that mine was much superior.

Hoskin: But how did you come to *have* such *fine* instruments?

Herschel: Well, it's rather a long story. My father, who was just a humble gardener in early life, was in many ways a most remarkable man. He gave us children a good training in music, and then in the evenings we would discuss philosophy, or study the stars, or something of that nature.

Hoskin: This was in Hanover.

Herschel: Yes. I didn't settle in England until 1757, after the French occupied Hanover, and my father advised me to leave.

Hoskin: You were then nineteen, and a refugee.

Herschel: Yes, but fortunately music is an international language. And I've never been afraid of hard work.

Hoskin: But what brought you to astronomy?

Herschel: Well, as a musician I had always been interested in the mathematical theory of harmony, and so I studied a well-known text on the subject, Dr Smith's *Harmonics*. Then I decided it might be interesting to read the same author's book on *Opticks*.

Hoskin: And this told you all about making telescopes.

Herschel: Yes, and something about astronomy as well.

Hoskin: But at this time astronomy was confined to the Sun, Moon and planets, wasn't it?

Herschel: Yes, the stars were not much more than points of light on a heavenly sphere, a kind of backcloth against which the planets moved. What little was known about them I learned rather from James Ferguson's book on *Astronomy*.

Hoskin: When was that?

Herschel: In 1773.

Hoskin: When you were in your middle thirties.

Herschel: Yes. Ferguson had more ideas than Smith, too. For example, he believed that God couldn't have made the universe just for man – after all, why should the Creator limit the richness of his creation? This is why we know there must be rational beings in every planetary system.

Hoskin: And presumably elsewhere in our own?

Herschel: That is so.

Hoskin: Even on the Moon?

Herschel: Yes, and I said as much in my first paper to the Royal Society on the lunar mountains. But the Astronomer Royal insisted I cut this passage out before the paper was published.

Hoskin: Presumably you wouldn't think there are rational beings on the Sun!

Herschel: Certainly on the Sun!

Hoskin: But surely it is much too hot there?

Herschel: This seems so when we first think about it. But what if the heat comes not from the body of the Sun itself but from a kind of blazing shell surrounding the Sun? Then the inhabitants of the Sun could be comfortably cool, just like mountaineers in summer – after all, they feel the heat less the nearer they climb to the Sun.

Hoskin: But all this is pure speculation.

Herschel: Well, how do you explain sunspots? I believe that these are really glimpses we get of this cool interior – gaps in

the blazing atmosphere. But in any case there *must* be
inhabitants simply because the Creator does not go about
his creating in half-hearted fashion.

Hoskin: What else did you learn from Ferguson?

Herschel: One thing I *didn't* learn was how far it is to the stars. All
Ferguson could say was how far it wasn't – it wasn't less
than four hundred thousand times the distance to the Sun.

Hoskin: How did he know this?

Herschel: Let us suppose we are walking down a country lane. We
come to a gap in the hedge, and we look through into a
field. We see the animals in the field; we see a clump of
trees a mile away; and we see hills in the distance. Then

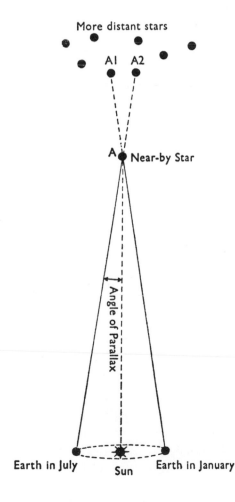

Astronomers measure the distance to a near-by star by observing changes in its position relative to distant background stars as the observer is carried with the Earth around the Sun. The nearer the star, the greater will be the observed changes

we walk on a little farther, until we come to another gap.
What do we see?

Hoskin: Well, the animals will look as though they have moved...

Herschel: Exactly, because we are now looking at them from a different direction.

Hoskin: Yes. The trees may look a little different, but probably not much – certainly not as much as the animals.

Herschel: That is so. The trees are farther away. And the distant hills?

Hoskin: I would expect them to look much the same as before.

Herschel: In other words, the things that are closest to you will have moved the most . . .

Hoskin: . . . you mean that if I took measurements I could work out from how much a thing seems to have moved, just how far away it is.

Herschel: Precisely. And this is how we calculate the distance to an inaccessible mountain, or to the equally inaccessible Moon.

Now, what about the distant hills which hadn't changed at all?

Hoskin: The gaps in the hedge couldn't have been far enough apart for measuring their distance.

Herschel: Yes, or perhaps you didn't do your measurements accurately enough. But if you knew both the distance between the gaps *and* the accuracy of your instruments, then you could say that the hills must be *at least* so many miles away. Otherwise you would have noticed some difference in how they appeared through the second gap. And this is how Ferguson knew the stars were *at least* four hundred thousand times farther away than the Sun. They looked exactly the same in winter, when the Earth is on one side of the Sun, as in the summer . . .

Hoskin: . . . when the Earth is away on the other side of the Sun. Quite a distance between the gaps in this particular hedge!

Herschel: Nearly two hundred million miles.

Hoskin: So we are back where we started, with the stars not much more than markers on a heavenly sphere.

Herschel: Yes, but don't despair, there is one other method we might try, to help calculate their distances. This time let us suppose we are out at night lost on the moors. We climb a hill, and lo and behold we see in the distance two shepherds' cottages, each with a light in the window. How do we decide which cottage is nearer?

Hoskin: Well, probably the one whose light looks brighter.

Herschel: And if we have reason to believe that the two shepherds are burning exactly the same lights?

Hoskin: Then we can be certain that the one that looks brighter is nearer.

Herschel: Yes, and if we have a way of actually measuring the brightness of each light we can even calculate how *much* nearer the brighter one is.

Hoskin: And you want to say that the stars are like these lamps, all equally bright in themselves, and that it is only because they are at different distances that some appear to us to be brighter than others? But this is a pretty wild assumption. What evidence could you possibly have to justify it?

Herschel: None at all, I'm afraid.

Hoskin: Why should the stars all be the same, and yet we know the planets are so different?

Herschel: But don't you understand that sometimes we *have* to make assumptions when we are studying nature, if we are to get anywhere at all. Only by assuming that the stars are all of roughly the same brightness could I begin to ask questions about what I call 'the construction of the heavens'.

Hoskin: You mean how the stars are spread out in space.

Herschel: Yes. Or rather, if I *didn't* make this assumption, I could ask the questions but I had no hope of answering them! But in any case, we cannot use the gaps-in-the-hedge technique we were talking about earlier, when we come to calculate the distances of the more remote stars. They are much too far away.

Hoskin: Before we leave the nearer stars, did you yourself try to make any gaps-in-the-hedge measurements?

Herschel: Oh certainly.

Hoskin: Weren't you afraid of biting off more than you could chew?

Herschel: That's my chief fault, I'm afraid.

Hoskin: But great observers had given their lives to this problem without success. And you had to earn your living as a musician.

Herschel: Yes, I was organist at Bath at the time, and I composed and conducted and took many pupils as well. But this still left much of the night free.

Hoskin: But why did you think you might succeed where others had failed?

Herschel: Well, they had run into all sorts of complications and difficulties. A new technique was needed.

I thought I could detect a slight difference in the position of a tree best if I noticed some distant hill just about in line with the tree. The distant hill would be, to all intents and purposes, fixed and so I would look for a change in position of the tree relative to this hill. In this way it would be much easier to pick out the tiny changes we are looking for.

Hoskin: But how could you find fixed points in the sky?

Herschel: Any faint star would do.

Hoskin: Because on *your* assumption any faint star *must* be very distant.

Herschel: Yes, so distant that for all practical purposes it would be fixed, like the hill was. By the way, it was Galileo who first suggested this technique. Now, you see, this meant looking for pairs of stars that look close together in the sky, one to be a faint distant star to serve as a fixed point of reference, and the other a bright near one whose change of position we hope to detect. I call such a pair a 'double star'.

Hoskin: But what if your assumption was wrong? What, for example, if the faint star is a kind of planet going round the bright one?

Herschel: I must admit this turned out to be the case in several of my doubles. But I only discovered this many years later, when the stars of each pair had had time to move round each other.

Hoskin: This must have been something of a disappointment as well as an exciting moment.

Herschel

Herschel at the age of 81, from the portrait by Artaud, 1819

Caroline Herschel, sister to William and for many years
his astronomical assistant, from a portrait by
Tielemann, 1829

William Herschel's 'large' 20-foot reflector, his most effective instrument, here shown as used in 1834 by his son John near the Cape of Good Hope

William Herschel's greatest telescope, with a tube over 40 feet long and nearly 5 feet in diameter. It proved difficult to manoeuvre, and the mirror was sensitive to temperature changes and its metal liable to tarnish

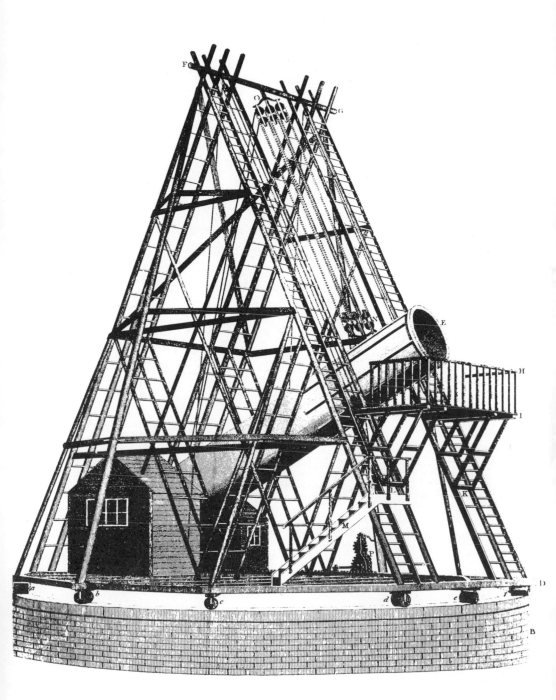

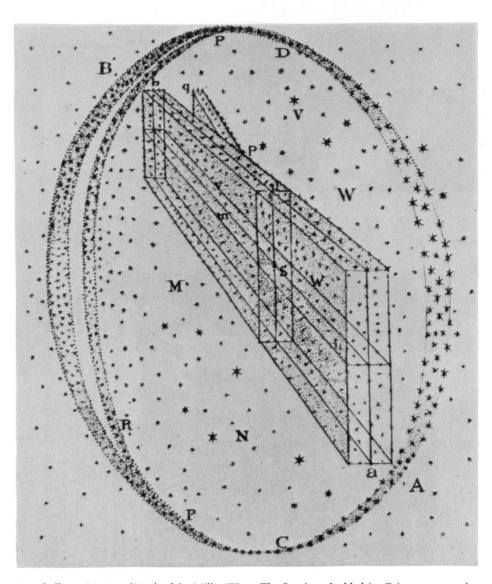

Herschel's explanation (1784) of the Milky Way. The Sun is embedded (at *S*) in a stratum of
stars which we observe projected against the sky in the form of the Milky Way

Photographs taken in 1908, 1915 and 1920 respectively showing the two stars of the pair known as Krueger 20 in orbit about their common centre of gravity. Herschel was the first astronomer to observe such movements, but he ignored the inference that the two stars are at virtually the same distance from us and therefore look different because they *are* different

The planetary nebula (now known as NGC 1514) which Herschel observed in 1790 and which convinced him that 'shining fluid' exists in addition to individual stars

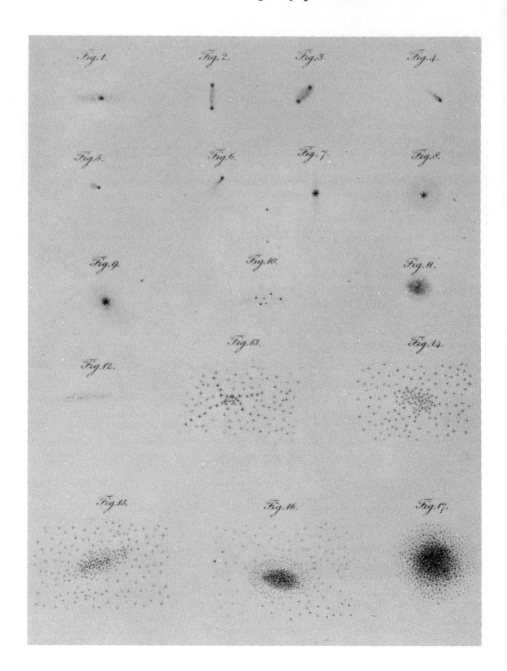

Sketches published in 1814 by Herschel to illustrate
his theory of the formation of stars and of the
development of ever-more-compressed systems of
stars as gravitational attraction operates over long
periods of time

Herschel: Well, there are always disappointments, but the exciting thing was that here we had the first undeniable proof that some sort of attractive forces were at work beyond our solar system, forces that were binding the stars to each other. Newton had assumed this, but he had no evidence.

Hoskin: And this discovery that some of your doubles were companion stars came as a complete surprise to you?

Herschel: Well, not exactly. In 1782 the Astronomer Royal had drawn my attention to a paper in the *Philosophical Transactions* by John Michell – a very remarkable paper – in which Michell argued that there were too *many* double stars in the sky for my explanation of them to be right.

Hoskin: You mean that on your argument a double star comes about by chance. The bright one just *happens* to be in line with the distant faint one.

Herschel: Yes. Michell claimed that this was occurring far too often, and therefore some of the doubles must consist of two stars going round each other.

Hoskin: These would look like double stars from whichever direction you looked at them; and not just because the two stars *happened* to be in line with you. But did not Michell write this *before* you got down to work?

Herschel: Yes, and he published another paper later in which he expressly forecast that some of my doubles would consist of two companion stars close together in space . . .

Hoskin: . . . and therefore useless for gaps-in-the-hedge measurements. So why did you persevere with double stars?

Herschel: Well, for one thing, he was talking about double stars in general, and his argument didn't necessarily apply to *every* double star. And I suppose the fact that I was well launched on this programme of work had something to do with it. Besides, how else could I hope to measure the distances of stars?

Hoskin: These later observations, when you found pairs of stars going round each other, must have put you in difficulties; because they meant not only that this particular technique had failed, but also that you now had examples where two stars are at the same distance from us in spite of the fact that one looks brighter than the other.

Herschel: That is so.

Hoskin: In other words, you had found examples to disprove your own assumption that the brighter stars are always the nearer ones.

Herschel: Well, I had always supposed that stars would differ to some extent, like one oak tree from another.

Hoskin: You mean not identical but very similar. You thought of the stars as members of a single group or species?

Herschel: Yes.

Hoskin: But the differences you had now discovered were much more striking. Doesn't this mean that you had to give up this whole method of estimating the distance of a star?

Herschel: Well, sometimes I needed these distances, and there was no other way of getting them, certainly for the more remote stars.

Hoskin: Do you mean to say that you persevered in spite of the fact that you had positive proof that your assumption was false?

Herschel: To give it up would have meant the end of my chief work in astronomy, the study of the construction of the heavens.

Hoskin: In view of what you've told me I find it surprising that you were regarded in your own time essentially as an observer, especially of the planets – as the discoverer of Uranus, for example.

Herschel: Yes, and even that discovery was made while I was searching the sky for double stars!

Still, one tangible result was that his gracious majesty awarded me a pension of £200, which allowed me to give up music and devote the rest of my life to astronomy. I was forty-three at the time, and I had so much to do.

Hoskin: Was £200 a year sufficient?

Herschel: Hardly, but in later years he added fifty pounds for my sister Caroline, who was my faithful assistant in all my work. I could always earn extra money by building and selling telescopes. And the king did grant me four thousand pounds to build my forty-foot telescope.

Hoskin: You mean a telescope with a barrel forty feet long?

Herschel: Roughly speaking, yes. The mirrors measured four feet across, and weighed up to a ton.

Hoskin: Yes, I have a picture of it here. Until very recently it would still have been the largest telescope in Britain. But why did you need to build such a large one?

Herschel: Well, Smith and Ferguson had long ago pointed out that to see a faint object you must collect enough light from it to register on the human eye. My telescope collected the light that fell on the mirror – an area of several square feet.

Hoskin: Did you build large telescopes from the start?

Herschel: Oh no, I began in a modest way by hiring small ones. But very soon I became ambitious, and then I ran into trouble.

First of all I had to learn how to construct a telescope once I had the mirror. Then I found that mirrors of the size I wanted were not to be bought, so I had to grind the rough disks into shape myself.

Hoskin: Did you have some craftsmen to teach you?

Herschel: No, I bought some secondhand tools from a neighbour, and learned from trial and error – but Dr Smith's book was a great help.

Hoskin: This was while you were still a musician.

Herschel: Yes. In the end the mirrors I needed were so large I couldn't even buy the rough disks, so I simply had to turn the basement of my house into a foundry.

One day my brother and I nearly lost our lives when the molten metal ran over the floor and the flagstones began to fly in all directions.

Hoskin: But it was worth it?

Herschel: Yes. With my great telescope I have looked farther into space than any human being ever did before me. I have observed stars whose light must have taken two million years to reach the earth.

Hoskin: How can you possibly know this?

Herschel: Well, we know light takes about eight minutes to reach us from the Sun. If the Sun were twice as far away, the light would take twice eight minutes to reach us; the Sun would then look one quarter of its present brightness – and of course we could still see it. Well, we go on like this, doubling the distance and doubling the time, until the Sun would be so far away we could barely see it, even with the great telescope. The time we have after all these doublings tells us how long the light would take to reach us from a star like the Sun at the far limit of the great telescope. These stars must have existed two million years ago – in fact, if they had *ceased* to exist a million years ago, we should still receive their light. But, after all, in astronomy millions of years are but moments and we have an eternity of past time at our disposal.

Hoskin: I must say this is an amazing leap forward from the time scale of Newton's contemporaries. They believed the world was less than six thousand years old. After all, the gap between his lifetime and yours was only twelve years.

Herschel: That is so.

Hoskin: Sir William, to return to your giant telescope, do you regard it as a complete success?

Herschel: Not altogether. I must admit it was something of a disappointment, although I discovered a new satellite of Saturn the first time that I used it. The trouble was that the mirror tarnished easily, and the machinery was awkward to manage. And of course it could show only a very small area of sky at any one time, so it was useless for a systematic survey of the entire heavens; I reckoned this would have taken me six centuries – not allowing for the time I needed to show it to distinguished visitors! Everyone from the King to the Archbishop of Canterbury came to see it.

Hoskin: But you had already examined the whole of the visible sky while you were still a musician, hadn't you?

Herschel: More than once, with small telescopes, first to get my bearings and then to collect double stars. But when I pursued the study of nebulae (these are milky patches of light in the sky that look something like comets), I needed a telescope much larger than I was using in those early days.

Hoskin: How did you come to be interested in nebulae?

Herschel: Well, as you know, we can see the great nebula in Orion with the unaided eye. I had read of it in Ferguson, and it was the very first object in the heavens I examined with a telescope. But my serious interest began in 1781 when a friend of mine sent me a catalogue that the French astronomer Messier had drawn up with over a hundred nebulae and clusters of stars.

Hoskin: You say nebulae *and* clusters of stars. Wouldn't a cluster of stars look like a milky streak in the sky if it was too far away for us to pick out the individual stars?

Herschel: Yes, and so the question was, are all nebulae merely star clusters disguised by distance, or are some formed of stars and others of something else?

Hoskin: But Messier's telescopes were not up to your standards.

Herschel: Quite so, and this was why I was so excited by the problem. I found I could detect stars in most of Messier's so-called nebulae, and so I could see no reason why all of them should not be simply clusters of stars.

Hoskin: You didn't examine each nebula in turn and satisfy yourself that it was made up of stars?

Herschel: No, how could one do that? Messier listed a hundred. I collected over two and a half thousand specimens – there's no end to them. So no one could examine them all, however big his telescope.

But the point was, we could see that *some* of the nebulae were made up of stars, so why not explain *all* of them in this way. It was up to anyone who disagreed to show why we needed to dream up some sort of luminous fluid of a nature quite unknown to us.

Hoskin: But wouldn't a large nebula like the nebula in Orion have to contain an enormous number of stars?

Herschel: There's no shortage of stars. I have myself seen hundreds of thousands passing through the field of view of my telescope in a matter of minutes.

Hoskin: But how about if you found that the Orion nebula changes visibly over a period of, say, ten or twenty years. An enormous collection of stars couldn't possibly alter so rapidly, so wouldn't this prove that the nebula was not made up of stars.

Herschel: That is quite true and in fact I later found changes in this very nebula. What finally made me change my mind was an observation I made in 1790. That November I found a star in the very middle of a kind of luminous atmosphere. Without the star I would have supposed the luminous atmosphere was a very distant collection; but with this bright one right in the middle – no! This was out of the question! I simply had to say that I had been mistaken and that some nebulae are not made up of stars.

Hoskin: But until then you thought an extensive nebula like the one in Orion must be a vast distant star system?

Herschel: Yes, perhaps even bigger than the Milky Way collection of stars, to which the Sun itself belongs.

Hoskin: But now the Orion nebula might be a luminous cloud comparatively close to us.

Herschel: Yes, indeed.

Hoskin: In other words, you couldn't any longer be sure that there are other star systems besides our own Milky Way. Well then, can you tell us something about our Milky Way system? You said the Sun is a member of it.

Herschel: It is in fact a layer of stars, and we, the Earth and Sun, are somewhere in the middle. I once thought I had mapped a cross-section of it.

Hoskin: How could you do that?

Herschel: Well, I wondered this myself, and then I realised I would have to make two assumptions. First of all, that my telescope could reach to the border in all directions – that was obviously necessary before I could start. Now if I look through my telescope I see an immense number of stars scattered about. To get a definite measurement then, I made a second assumption, that the stars in the Milky Way are spread out at fairly regular intervals . . .

Hoskin: Something like soldiers drawn up on parade?

Herschel: Yes. By and large it is surely reasonable to suppose that the more stars there are in any particular direction, the farther it is to the border.

Hoskin: But of course the second assumption is not true – the stars are *clustered* in some places, like the Pleiades, whereas in other places we see very few.

Herschel: Yes, the assumption is not absolutely true; and I allowed for this. I made ten counts and took the average.

A cross-section of the Milky Way star system, as published by Herschel in 1785. The star near the centre represents the Sun

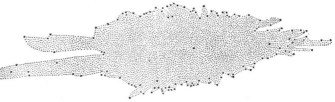

Hoskin: This is the start of the modern technique of star counts.

Herschel: Is that so? At the time, the question really was whether the assumption was true enough for my purposes. I'm afraid that after some years I decided it was not; and so I had to tear up my map of our star system.

Hoskin: But it had been published by that time. I've seen your map in any number of Victorian text books! But to come back to your nebulae: having collected these thousands, what did you do?

Herschel: I was perfectly happy to be a kind of natural historian of the heavens, a collector of specimens, provided that they were to be the raw material for understanding the construction of the heavens. The great problem was to get the nebulae sorted out by some reasonable method: to see why some were different from others.

Hoskin: I suppose part of the answer must lie in the fact that we don't always look at them from the same angle, and that some are nearer than others.

Herschel: But there is more to it than that. The fact that you have a cluster of stars at all suggests that there is some force at work pulling them in towards each other. I concluded that the ones that were tightly packed were so because an attractive force had been at work on them for longer – in other words, they were the older ones.

Eventually I came to understand that the stars have a history, and that although our own lives are so very short we can learn about that history if we think of the way we learn about the growth of an oak tree. An oak tree may grow for a thousand years, but we learn about it not by watching for changes in a single tree – life is too short – but by going into a forest one day and looking at the oak trees at the different stages of life: young saplings, mature trees, and so on. From the forest we learn in a single day how one oak tree develops over a thousand years. And from my catalogue we can do the same for nebulae.

Hoskin: But what happened to this theory when you discovered that a luminous atmosphere can exist?

Herschel: Well, it seemed to me, looking at that bright star with its halo around it, that the atmosphere must be condensing down to form the star.

Hoskin: The star was actually growing?

Herschel: Yes. And so I extended my theory to allow for this. I began with a vast, thinly spread, luminous atmosphere, and then I showed how the denser parts began to form into stars. And then how the stars would begin to cluster. I ended with examples of tightly packed clusters of stars.

Hoskin: Clusters in their old age!

Herschel: Yes. But unfortunately, as you were saying earlier, now if I looked at a nebula I couldn't be sure if it was a cloud of luminous atmosphere, or another vast milky way like our own with its millions of stars.

Hoskin: Your earlier theories certainly came in for some hard knocks later in your career! Your map of the Milky Way, your attempts to measure the distances of stars, and now this!

Herschel: One must expect such things to happen if one delves into great problems. During my life as an astronomer I have tried to maintain a proper balance between observation and theory. If you build a fanciful world of your own, without making observations, you can't expect this to be the actual world of nature. On the other hand, if you simply pile up observations without drawing conclusions from them and without speculating about them, then you have wasted your time. And I have tried never to waste my time.

Hoskin: Sir William, one final point. Sir Isaac Newton seemed to think that God will never let the planets fall into the Sun – He will step in from time to time to keep the solar system going like clockwork. Yet for you there is change everywhere.

Herschel: God preserves his universe in ways that we can only glimpse. But parts of it change with the passage of time.

So the Milky Way itself, as it breaks up into smaller clusters of stars, suffers the ravages of time. It cannot last for ever, nor can its past be infinite.

Hoskin: I was particularly interested in two things that came out in our conversation.

The first was his theory of how the star-systems develop with the passage of time. This was one of the first important examples of an evolutionary theory in science. The other was the way in which Sir William refused to abandon his useful hypothesis about the stars being equally bright just because it was contradicted by some evidence. It seems to me that we are often tempted to take too crude a view of science, and imagine the scientist being enslaved by facts – as though an hypothesis must be thrown out the moment there's trouble. I remember a modern astrophysicist saying to me that one research student of his had never made any progress because every time he had an idea he immediately saw reasons why it must be wrong – and so he dropped the idea before he had given it a fair trial.

Sir William has shown us how in science, as in life, we sometimes have to live with contradictions.

4   Darwin: *The evolution principle*

In the seventeenth century a wave of enthusiasm for collecting species of living things swept Europe. This rich harvest of factual knowledge raised deep issues. It was known from the book of *Genesis* that God had created each species at the beginning of the world; and the way in which each species is so exquisitely equipped for life in the particular conditions in which it is found was proof of the supreme skill of its Maker and of his concern for the welfare of his creation. But why do we find so very many species, and how are we to make sense of the relationship of one species to another that we express when we speak of two species belonging to the same genus?

Here and there, biologists were toying with an exciting idea which, if true, would mean that many of these species-problems were false ones. Perhaps species were not fixed for all time, but could change. After all, as Erasmus Darwin pointed out in his *Zoonomia* (1794–6), breeders of horses and dogs bring about new varieties; why should not similar, but more radical, changes occur in nature, perhaps by the efforts of the animals to meet needs imposed by their conditions of life?

The trouble was that, so far, the evidence was simply not strong enough to *compel* biologists to admit that species change under natural conditions. And furthermore there was no obvious *cause* to bring about such changes, no natural selector to take the place of the horse-breeder or pigeon-fancier who chooses which animals to mate and which of the young to rear. In the end it was Erasmus's own grandson, Charles Darwin, who proved the *fact* of change with a magnificent wealth of evidence, and who provided a mechanism to take the place of the horse-breeder.

Charles was born in 1809, and was educated at Shrewsbury School. He studied medicine at Edinburgh Uni-

versity, but soon gave this up in favour of Cambridge
where he prepared to become a clergyman. Although he
afterwards claimed to have had little benefit from his
formal education, at Cambridge especially he became in
his spare time an enthusiastic geologist and natural
historian, and in 1831 he was recommended to Captain
Fitzroy of H.M.S. *Beagle* as a suitable naturalist to take
on a voyage around the world. The voyage took five
years, and it gave Darwin a wonderful opportunity to
study geology and wild life on a grand scale, particularly
in South America. On his return to England Darwin
began to assemble evidence relating to changes in species;
and he began to search for the causes of these changes.

In 1839 Darwin married, and he and his wife settled at
Downe in Kent where he was to live, an amateur
scientist of private means, until his death in 1882. Shortly
before his wedding he happened to read for amusement
Malthus on *Population*, and noted particularly the passage
where Malthus explains how a human population would,
unless checked, multiply in numbers at every generation.
But the food supply, Malthus reckoned, increased at an
altogether slower rate, with the result that at each
generation more children are born than can be fed with
the available food, so there must be a struggle for survival. In this struggle between individuals, and even
between species, those with advantages might cause the
rest to become extinct.

The jigsaw now began to fall into place, but Darwin
knew he would be treading on scientific as well as
religious toes, and he must marshal his evidence with
extreme care. He wrote out a brief sketch, then a longer
one, and finally embarked on a full-scale work. This was
well under way when in 1858 he was dismayed to receive
from a Mr Wallace in the Far East an essay which could
well have been a summary of his own work. What
should he do? After consulting his friends, he published
Wallace's essay and something of his own in the same
journal, and at once set to work to write a summary,
itself of book length, of the full-scale work he had

originally planned. *On the Origin of Species by means of Natural Selection, or the preservation of favoured races in the struggle for life* was published in 1859.

Like all epoch-making works in science, it answered old questions – or showed them to have been badly put – only to raise a host of new ones. Biology would never be the same, and neither would theology, for as the years went by Darwin became more and more frank about his conviction that man had evolved like any other species of animal.

Meanwhile, in spite of poor health, Darwin was putting out a succession of new works and revised editions of old ones – but, strange to relate, he was losing faith in the mechanism he had himself proposed as the cause of changes in species. He grew to think that the characteristics of a child tend to be a compromise between the characteristics of the two parents, and that therefore a parent can only partially hand on to a child an advantage the parent has had in the struggle for survival.

In fact Darwin had been right in the first place, and the solution to his anxieties about inherited characteristics lay in a paper published in 1866 by an Augustinian monk, Gregor Mendel, which was to provide the foundations of modern genetics. But Mendel's work was recognised only after Darwin was dead.

In his early manhood Darwin was capable of considerable feats of endurance in South American expeditions, but for many years now he has had to nurse his health. He is probably suffering from an obscure disease contracted in South America, one that leads to a feeling of lassitude and loss of drive. But the disease is not understood, and he is widely suspected of mere hypochondria. As a result he lives in the shelter of his large and devoted family, rarely venturing into the outside world and avoiding social contacts. He is fortunate in having been provided for by his father, so that he has never had to struggle to earn his own daily bread; instead he has enjoyed indefinite leisure in which to pursue his elaborate researches.

As a person he is simple to the point of naivety. His wife said: 'He is the most open transparent man I ever saw, and every word expresses his real thoughts.' He has a sense of fun, and is exceedingly thoughtful and generous. He tends to avoid controversy and prefers others to fight his battles for him, but he has high principles and an ability to see many sides to a question.

Hoskin: Why are there so many species of animals and plants, and why do some species have so much in common with each other? The eighteenth-century answers to these questions took it for granted that species do not change. God, it was said, expressed his unlimited powers by specially creating every possible species. And since these species were arranged in a single unbroken chain from the lowest and most primitive to the highest, man, each species of course had much in common with its near neighbours on the chain.

But these answers were never completely satisfactory. Why did God allow suffering? Did not the fossil record show that many species had become extinct? And the history of the Earth seemed to be on a far grander scale than the Old Testament account implied. But on the other hand, if you wanted to say that species change, could you be sure of this? After all, what could cause them to change, and in any case was there enough time?

The man who proved that species do change, and contributed greatly to our understanding of what causes this to happen, was Charles Darwin.

Mr Darwin, it's an extraordinary fact that most of the ideas that went into your theory of evolution are to be found in the writings of your own grandfather. How much did his work influence you?

Darwin: I read my grandfather's book *Zoonomia* when I was young, and I admired it greatly. But when I read it a second time after an interval of ten or fifteen years, I was disappointed in it – the proportion of speculation was so large in comparison with the facts he gave. In the same way a fellow undergraduate told me of my grandfather's French contemporary, Lamarck, and his views on evolution; but as far as I can judge this had no effect on me.

Hoskin: But the idea of evolution was in the air?

Darwin: Well it had certainly been discussed, but I never came across a serious naturalist who believed that species do change. But I think it is true that a great many well-observed facts were stored in the minds of naturalists, ready to take their proper places as soon as a theory was explained to account for them.

Hoskin: What was it like, having a famous grandfather?

Darwin: Oh, he died before I was born. It was my father who dominated the family. He was the largest man I ever saw, twenty-four stone of him. But his mind was not scientific. He didn't try to express his knowledge under general laws.

Hoskin: And your mother?

Darwin: She died when I was eight, and I can hardly remember anything about her. It was a year after that that I went to Dr Butler's great school at Shrewsbury, where I stayed until I was sixteen. But the school as a means of education to me was simply a blank – the studies were strictly classical.

Hoskin: Latin and Greek? From what you say it sounds as though you didn't come top of the class.

Darwin: When I left the school all my masters thought me a very ordinary boy, rather below average. And my father once said to me, 'You care for nothing but shooting, dogs, and rat-catching – you will be a disgrace to yourself and all your family.'

Hoskin: You had no scientific interests at school?

Darwin: I collected minerals and insects – *dead* insects, as my sister told me it was wrong to kill insects just to make a collection. And towards the end of my school life I helped my brother in his chemical experiments – he had a laboratory with proper apparatus in the tool-house in the garden. This was the best part of my education, though Dr Butler didn't approve at all, and it showed me, practically, the meaning of experimental science.

Hoskin: What did your father make of all this?

Darwin: Well, I was doing no good at school, so when I was sixteen he sent me to Edinburgh University to study medicine. But I felt sure that he would leave me enough money to live on, and so I didn't make any great effort to learn medicine.

Hoskin: Did you find Edinburgh an improvement on Shrewsbury?

Darwin: No, the instruction was entirely by lectures, and these were intolerably dull. Dr Duncan's lectures on drugs at eight o'clock on a winter's morning are something fearful to remember. Anyhow, human anatomy disgusted me.

Hoskin: Not a promising start to a medical career!

Darwin: No. And so when my father saw that I didn't like the thought of being a physician, he proposed that I should become a clergyman. This meant I must take a degree at one of the English universities.

Hoskin: Then your years at Edinburgh were a complete waste of time?

Darwin: No, I made friends with several young men fond of the natural sciences. I used to go with one of them to collect animals in the tidal pools, and I dissected them as well as I could. And during my second year I attended Professor Robert Jameson's lectures on geology and zoology; but they were incredibly boring. The sole effect they produced on me was the determination never, as long as I lived, to read a book on geology or in any way to study the subject.

Hoskin: How did you react to your father's proposal that you become a clergyman?

Darwin: I asked for some time to consider. But as I did not then doubt the strict and literal truth of every word in the Bible, I soon persuaded myself that our creed must be fully accepted. So I went to Cambridge, early in 1828.

Hoskin: I hope you had better luck with the teaching there!

Darwin: No, I'm afraid my three years in Cambridge were wasted as completely as my time at Edinburgh and at school – as far as the academical studies were concerned.

Hoskin: You studied what, classics . . . ?

Darwin: . . . and mathematics, and William Paley's books, which we all *had* to study. The logic of Paley's reasoning appealed to me.

Hoskin: Paley gives the old argument for the existence of God, doesn't he? From the evidence of design in nature.

Darwin: Yes, Paley says that if we find a watch on the ground and pick it up and examine it, we soon convince ourselves that the watch had a maker who designed it for telling the time – even though we never actually saw him at work. In the same way, he argues, if we examine an eye we find it is wonderfully designed for seeing, and so must have a designer, who is God.

This argument – which then completely convinced me – was the basis for the then accepted belief that all species had remained fixed and immutable since their creation.

Hoskin: Did you go to any of the courses, in view of your experiences in Edinburgh?

Darwin: Not many, but I did attend John Henslow's lectures on botany. Henslow used to take his pupils on field excursions, and lectured on the rarer plants or animals which were seen. These excursions were delightful.

Hoskin: And very forward looking for their day.

Darwin: Yes. But nothing I did at Cambridge gave me so much pleasure as collecting beetles. It was the mere passion for collecting. I remember one day I tore off some old bark from a tree and saw two rare beetles there. I seized one in each hand – but then I saw a third and new kind, which I couldn't bear to lose. So I popped the one which I held in my right hand into my mouth! Alas, it ejected some intensely acrid fluid, which burnt my tongue, so that I was forced to spit the beetle out – and I lost it and the third one as well.

Hoskin: But at least you held onto one of them!

Darwin: Yes! But at Cambridge what influenced my career more than anything else was my friendship with Professor Henslow. I took long walks with him most days, and some of the dons called me 'the man who walks with Henslow'. It was he who persuaded me to study geology in my last two terms in Cambridge, and it was he who asked Professor Sedgwick to let me accompany him on his geological investigations in North Wales.

Sedgwick's very first conversation with me made a big impression on my mind. I told him of a tropical shell which a labourer claimed he had found in an old gravel pit near Shrewsbury. But Sedgwick said at once that it must have been thrown away by someone into the pit – and he added that if it had really been embedded there it would be the greatest misfortune to geology.

Hoskin: Because it would disprove the current theories.

Darwin: Yes. But I was utterly astonished at Sedgwick not being delighted at so wonderful a fact as a tropical shell being found near the surface in the middle of England. Nothing before had ever made me realise that science consists in grouping facts so that general laws or conclusions may be drawn from them.

Hoskin: And one could go on to say that a fact only becomes a *scientific* fact when it is relevant to some theory – when it tells for or against some hypothesis. And one exception may be devastating.

Darwin: Yes. How odd it is that anyone should not see that all observation must be for or against some view if it is to be of any use.

Well, on returning home from Wales I found a letter from Henslow telling me that Captain Fitzroy of H.M.S. *Beagle* was willing to give up part of his own cabin to any young man who would volunteer to go with him as naturalist on a voyage round the world. Fitzroy wanted someone to gather evidence to help defend the strict and

Darwin

Charles Darwin, photographed in his middle 60s

One of several cartoons published of Darwin.
This appeared in the *London Sketch Book*

Thomas Henry Huxley, the staunch friend whom Darwin called
'My general agent'

'Soapy Sam' Wilberforce, Bishop of Oxford, whose ill judged attack
on Darwin's theory at the 1860 meeting of the British Association for
the Advancement of Science brought a stinging rebuff from Huxley

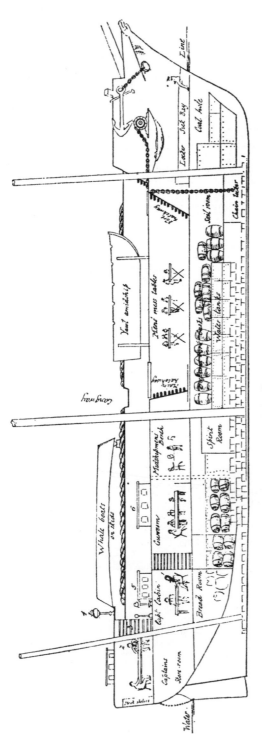

H.M.S. Beagle 1832

1 Mr Darwin's seat in Capt. Cabin
2   "   "   "   " Poop   "
3   "   "   drawers   "   "
4 Azimuth Compass
5 Captain's Skylight
6 Guns.

Drawing of the *Beagle*, showing (1) Darwin's seat in the Captain's Cabin, (2) Darwin's seat in the Poop Cabin, and (3) the drawers where Darwin's specimens were kept. Drawn in later life by Philip Gidley King, midshipman on the *Beagle* and a frequent companion of Darwin on shore. From *Charles Darwin's Diary of the Voyage of H.M.S. "Beagle"*, edited by Nora Barlow

The *Beagle* laid ashore at the mouth of the river Santa Cruz, from Robert FitzRoy's
Narrative of the Surveying Voyages of HMS Adventure and Beagle, vol. ii (1839)

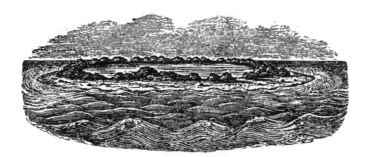

View of a circular atoll of coral-reefs (Whit-Sunday Island, South Pacific Ocean), from
Darwin's *Structure and Distribution of Coral Reefs* (1842).
Darwin showed that such atolls could not be reefs built on the rims of submerged volcanic
craters, as generally believed, and argued instead that such a coral reef must have grown up
as an existing island slowly subsided into the sea

literal truth of every statement in the Bible.

Hoskin: But were you free to go? Weren't you studying for the Church?

Darwin: Yes, and my father thought that to go on this wild scheme would be disreputable to my character as a clergyman. You know, the voyage of the *Beagle* was by far the most important event in my life and determined my whole career. Yet it depended on my uncle offering to drive me thirty miles to Shrewsbury to talk with my father.

Hoskin: And your father gave his consent.

Darwin: In the kindest manner.

Hoskin: How long did the voyage last?

Darwin: Five years, most of which were spent along the shores of South America. I have always felt that I owe to the voyage the first real training or education of my mind. My powers of observation were improved – but far more important was the investigation of the geology of all the places 'we visited, because in geology you have to reason.

Hoskin: How do you mean?

Darwin: Well, when you first examine a new district the chaos of rocks seems hopeless. But if you record the layers and the nature of the rocks and fossils at many points, reasoning it out and predicting what you will find elsewhere, you discover that the general structure then becomes more or less intelligible.

Hoskin: You mean that you began to form hypotheses on the evidence that you first came across, and then you tested these hypotheses against the later evidence?

Darwin: Yes. And I studied the first volume of Lyell's *Principles of Geology* which Henslow had given me – though he warned me on no account to accept Lyell's *views*.

Hoskin: He wanted you to use the book merely as a compendium of facts.

Darwin: Yes.

Hoskin: I suppose he didn't like Lyell's views because Lyell insisted that the Earth as we know it has been formed over millions of years, and simply by the forces we see at work today. No divine interventions, no great up-heavals, only *continuous* processes – ones that science can investigate.

Darwin: Exactly. For example, Lyell claimed that long lines of inland cliffs have been formed and great valleys excavated by the agencies which we *still* see at work. But many geologists found this a great difficulty, because the mind cannot grasp the full meaning of even a million years.

In the same way the main cause of our unwillingness to admit that one species has given birth to other and distinct species is that we are always slow in admitting great changes of which we do not see the steps. The mind cannot add up the full effects of many slight variations accumulated during an almost infinite number of generations.

Now on the *Beagle* I studied Lyell's book *carefully*. And the very first district I examined showed me clearly the wonderful superiority of his method of treating geology.

Hoskin: And soon you were convinced that Lyell was right that the time-scale of the Earth is to be measured in millions of years.

Darwin: Yes.

Hoskin: But what led you to believe that species had changed? After all, Lyell himself was opposed to this, wasn't he?

Darwin: Yes, and he maintained this position for thirty years, but gave it up on reading my work – something which I think is without parallel in the records of science.

Hoskin: Yes, most scientists would rather die than alter their minds on a fundamental question! But what led you to believe that species change?

Darwin: Well, during the voyage of the *Beagle* I was deeply impressed by a number of things: by discovering in one place great fossil animals covered with armour like that on the existing armadillos; by the way in which closely allied animals replace one another as you proceed south-wards over the continent of South America; and by the South American character of most of the animals of the Galapagos Islands; and more particularly by the way in which they differ slightly on each island of the group.

Hoskin: Could we take these in turn. First you found great animal fossils which looked like existing animals *except* that they were far bigger in size. And you wondered why they had died and others so similar were still living.

Then, in addition to these examples of similar animals separated in time, you found many examples of similar animals separated in *space* – as you travelled south the species changed *gradually* from place to place. And you wondered why this should be so. And the most striking example of this you found in some islands hundreds of miles out in the Pacific Ocean. There the animals were *nearly* the same on each island, but not *quite*.

Darwin: Yes. Unfortunately until my investigation was nearly complete it never occurred to me that on islands only a few miles apart and with the same physical conditions the animals would be dissimilar. Yet in the thirteen species of groundfinches you can trace a nearly perfect series of steps from a beak that is extraordinarily thick to one that's so fine you could compare it to a warbler. And if you show the Spaniards a tortoise from one of the islands they can tell you at once which island it has come from, simply from the form of its body, the shape of its scale and its general size. It was clear that facts like these could only be explained on the supposition that species gradually become modified.

Finches of the Galapagos Islands, as illustrated in Darwin's *Journal of Researches* (1839)

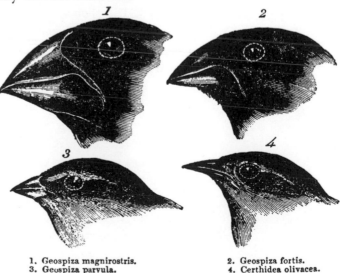

1. Geospiza magnirostris.
2. Geospiza fortis.
3. Geospiza parvula.
4. Certhidea olivacea.

The subject haunted me. And so a few months after my return to England, I opened my first note book for facts relating to the origin of species, and I never ceased working on this for the next twenty years.

Hoskin: But what about the question of what *causes* species to change?

Darwin: And the question of why organisms of every kind are so beautifully adapted to their habits of life – a woodpecker to climb trees, or a seed to be scattered by hooks or plumes. Until these could be explained it seemed to me almost useless to try to prove by indirect evidence that species have been modified. And they couldn't be explained by the will of the organisms, or the action of the surrounding conditions, as some writers have tried to do – such as my grandfather, and his French contemporary Lamarck.

Hoskin: Because, for example, conditions on each of those islands you visited were exactly the same, while at the same time the species of finches and tortoises were *different*. So somehow the barrier of a mile or two of water must have been enough to allow each species to develop its own characteristics.

Darwin: Yes.

Hoskin: So what did you do?

Darwin: Well, about fifteen months after I had opened my first notebook, I happened to read for amusement Thomas Malthus's *Essay on Population* and . . .

Hoskin: Excuse me. Malthus maintained, didn't he, that at each generation a population – human, animal or plant – tends to multiply. For example if, on the average, two human parents have four children, then the population will double with each generation, *provided* the children survive. And after eight more generations you would have more than a thousand to take the place of the first parents.

Darwin: Yes, and he pointed out that in fact the food supplies increase much more slowly . . .

Hoskin: So that there is a constant check on the population.

Darwin: Yes. Now from my long-continued observations of the habits of animals and plants I was well able to appreciate the struggle for existence which everywhere goes on. And it struck me at once that under these circumstances *favourable* variations, however small, would tend to be preserved, and unfavourable ones destroyed. The result of this would be the formation of new species.

I called this process 'natural selection' and the result is the survival of the fittest.

Hoskin: Could we see if I've got this clear? Let's suppose we have a lot of giraffes. Then some will of course be taller than others. But there is not enough food for them all, so the shorter giraffes go hungry and die, while the taller ones can reach higher in the trees for food and so manage to survive and have young ones.

But these young will tend to be tall like their parents – taller, that is, than the average giraffe *used* to be. In this way the average height will increase – and so the later giraffes will be different from their ancestors – in time perhaps so different that we would call it a *new species*.

Darwin: That would be one simple example, yes.

Hoskin: So now you had an idea of what *causes* species to change.

Darwin: Yes.

Hoskin: And this was a grand idea of yours, affecting every living species.

Darwin: Yes. So I was anxious to avoid prejudice. And it wasn't until 1842 that I first allowed myself the satisfaction of writing a very brief abstract of my theory in pencil. Two years later I enlarged it to 230 pages.

Hoskin: You were married by this time?

Darwin: Yes, I was married in 1839. My dear wife has been my greatest blessing, without her my life would have been miserable – because of my ill-health.

Hoskin: Did you suffer from ill-health during the *Beagle* voyage?

Darwin: No – then I could ride a horse for ten hours at a time, and I thought nothing of sleeping rough for weeks on end. But since my return I have lost much of my time through illness. This is why my wife and I have lived such a retired life. You see, I found that after meeting friends my health always suffered from the excitement, which brought on violent shivering and vomiting attacks. I get exhausted now by seeing and talking with anyone for even an hour – except my wife and children.

Hoskin: Yes, I must be careful not to tire you.

Darwin: Well, I have nothing to report during the rest of my life, except the publication of my various books.

Hoskin: You had time to write many books because you never had to go out and earn your living?

Darwin: Fortunately no – my father always provided for me. And so my chief enjoyment, and my sole employment throughout life, has been scientific work.

Hoskin: The world has left you to get on with it in peace.

Darwin: Yes, and the excitement of it makes me forget my daily discomfort.

Hoskin: We got as far as the longer sketch of your theory.

Darwin: Yes, that was in 1844. Twelve years later Lyell advised me to write out my views pretty fully, and I began to do so on a much larger scale than was afterwards published in my *Origin of Species*.

But my plans were all upset in 1858 when Mr Alfred Russel Wallace, who was then in the Malay Archipelago, sent me an essay which contained exactly the same theory as mine.

Hoskin: What a dreadful thing to happen to you, and after twenty years' work on the theory! What did you do?

Darwin: With many misgivings, and on the advice of friends, I had Mr Wallace's essay published jointly with some pieces of mine. But they didn't excite much attention – which shows how necessary it is that any new view should be explained at length.

Hoskin: But I expect the shock of Wallace's essay galvanised you into action.

Darwin: Yes! After thirteen months and ten days of hard labour my *Origin of Species* was published in November 1859.

Hoskin: Mr Darwin, one of the most important implications of your theory is that man has animals for his ancestors.

Darwin: That is true.

Hoskin: Did you make this plain in your book?

Darwin: At the time when I first became convinced that species change I could not avoid believing that man must come under the same law. And so I collected notes on the subject – for my own satisfaction, not for a long time with any intention of publishing. But in order that no honourable man should accuse me of concealing my views, I added in my book on *The Origin of Species* that 'light will be thrown on the origin of man and his history'.

Hoskin: What? You mean to say, only *one* sentence in the whole book?

Darwin: Yes – but of course when I found that many naturalists fully accepted my doctrine of the evolution of species, I worked up my notes into a special treatise on the origin of man. It was published in 1871 as *The Descent of Man*.

Hoskin: And that was no less then twelve years after *The Origin of Species*. And meanwhile friends like Thomas Henry Huxley were fighting your battles for you.

Darwin: That is true. I used to call Huxley 'my general agent', and others called him my 'bulldog'.

After the *Origin* was published awful fights raged in the newspapers and drawing-rooms. There was one pitched battle at a meeting in Oxford – I'm glad I wasn't there; I should have been overwhelmed, with my health in the state it was. But Huxley answered the Bishop of Oxford capitally – whereas I would as soon have died as tried to answer the bishop in such an assembly.

Hoskin: What did the bishop say?

Darwin: It seems he assured his listeners that there was nothing in the idea of evolution; and he asked Huxley whether he claimed descent from a monkey through his grandfather or his grandmother.

Hoskin: What did Huxley say to that?

Darwin: He said he would prefer to have a miserable ape for a grandfather, rather than a man who employed his great talents to introduce ridicule into a grave scientific discussion.

Hoskin: But was the bishop a scientist?

Darwin: No, but he was the spokesman for scientists.

Hoskin: There was no question of a fight with the scientists on one side and the bishop on the other?

Darwin: By no means. But it is true that the old argument for the existence of a personal God – the argument from design in nature, which used to seem so conclusive to me (you know, Paley's argument), fails now that the law of natural selection has been discovered.

Hoskin: You mean that giraffes have long necks, not because God decided to make them that way, but because long necks have helped their ancestors to survive periods of famine.

Darwin: Yes. There seems to be no more *design* in the variability of living things and in the action of natural selection than in the ways the wind blows.

Hoskin: But you are not saying that because one argument for the existence of God proves unsatisfactory, therefore God does not exist?

Darwin: No. But I cannot pretend to throw the least light on such abstruse problems. It is not in our power to solve the mystery of the beginning of all things; and I for one must be content to admit I do not know. I am agnostic.

Hoskin: Mr Darwin, this caution seems to me to be characteristic of your scientific work also. You took twenty years to publish your theory of evolution, and twelve more to make clear its implications for man. And yet your caution hasn't prevented you from bringing about a revolution in thought. How is this?

Darwin: It is hard to understand. My power to follow a purely abstract train of thought is very limited. And my memory is hazy – and I've no great quickness of wit which is so remarkable in some clever men, like Huxley. But I don't think it's true to say, like some of my critics, 'Oh, he's a good observer but he's no power of reasoning.' After all, *The Origin of Species* is one long argument from beginning to end. And I notice things which easily escape attention, and observe them carefully. And I've always had the strongest desire to understand or explain whatever I observed – to group all facts under some general laws – though I've tried always to give up any hypothesis as soon as the facts are clearly against it.

But it's truly surprising that with such moderate abilities I should have influenced the beliefs of scientific men on some important points.

Hoskin: Mr Darwin, I hope we have not tired you too much.

others; it follows, that the amount of organic change in the fossils of consecutive formations probably serves as a fair measure of the lapse of actual time. A number of species, however, keeping in a body might remain for a long period unchanged, whilst within this same period, several of these species, by migrating into new countries and coming into competition with foreign associates, might become modified; so that we must not overrate the accuracy of organic change as a measure of time. During early periods of the earth's history, when the forms of life were probably fewer and simpler, the rate of change was probably slower; and at the first dawn of life, when very few forms of the simplest structure existed, the rate of change may have been slow in an extreme degree. The whole history of the world, as at present known, although of a length quite incomprehensible by us, will hereafter be recognised as a mere fragment of time, compared with the ages which have elapsed·since the first creature, the progenitor of innumerable extinct and living descendants, was created.

In the distant future I see open fields for far more important researches. Psychology will be based on a new foundation, that of the necessary acquirement of each mental power and capacity by gradation. Light will be thrown on the origin of man and his history.

Authors of the highest eminence seem to be fully satisfied with the view that each species has been independently created. To my mind it accords better with what we know of the laws impressed on matter by the Creator, that the production and extinction of the past and present inhabitants of the world should have been due to secondary causes, like those determining the birth and death of the individual. When I view all beings not as special creations, but as the lineal descendants of some few beings which lived long before the

A page from the first edition (1859) of *The Origin of Species*, with the remark on the implications of the book for the origin of man

Mr Darwin spoke of influencing the beliefs of scientific men on some important points. But really he did much more than that. What he did was to give us a new basis for understanding life; he showed that living species are the result of natural causes acting to bring about changes *gradually*, over immense periods of time. *Gradually.*

There are no sudden leaps from one period to another, from one species to another, not even from animals to man. There are no sudden interventions by God, no sudden disastrous floods or frosts or upheavals. Everything happens gradually, in a way science can comprehend. Once we have this clear in our minds we can admit that in science, too, things happen gradually.

Darwin himself was hesitant in the face of scientific objections which we now know to have been mistaken, and came to lose confidence in his own cause for evolution. But if he was uncertain *how* evolution happens he certainly convinced the world *that* evolution happens, and that evolution is the fundamental law of life.

After all, if he had not raised as many questions as he answered, he would not have been the great scientist he was.

Pasteur: *The uses of science*

Today the union between science and technology is very close. Many practical needs are answered through the application of theories originally created by disinterested scientific curiosity; on the other hand, not only the tools of the scientist but often the very problems he studies are the results of man's attempts to impose his will on the world around him.

It was not always like this. In the middle ages, for example, technology and theory were almost completely separate; advances in technology, such as the application of water-power, developed out of experience, by trial and error, rather than from the application of any theory. By the seventeenth century the advantages science and technology had to offer each other were well understood, and the scientist had learned from the technologist the desire to control nature. But not for another two hundred years did the advantages become an established reality. They are nowhere better illustrated than in the work of Louis Pasteur.

Pasteur was born in 1822, the son of a tanner in the little French town of Dôle. He was hardworking though not outstanding as a schoolboy; artistically he was very gifted. At the École Normale in Paris he specialised in physics and chemistry. When he was only twenty-five he showed his clarity of thought and his genius as an experimenter when he solved a long-standing problem essentially by dividing a pile of crystals into two parts on the basis of their lack of symmetry and noting that the two piles had different optical properties.

In 1848 Pasteur was appointed to teach chemistry at the University of Strassburg, and married the following year. Soon his interests in the optical properties of non-symmetric compounds led him to the field of study in which he was to become great, that of small living organisms; for he had reason to believe that only living agents could produce non-symmetric compounds that had the optical properties noted earlier. The presence of such compounds immediately led him to expect the presence of living agents.

In 1854 he transferred to the University of Lille, where he was expected to interest himself in the industries of the region, which included the manufacture of beer. He was asked to help explain the contamination that sometimes occurred during fermentation, and in samples of fermenting beer he discovered substances that again had singular optical properties. At this time the action of yeast in fermentation was believed to be purely chemical. But for Pasteur the optical properties betrayed the presence of living organisms: the yeast was not dead but alive. To begin with, Pasteur was following a hunch. He believed he was right, but now he must try to prove it. Pasteur's ingenuity and thoroughness as an experimenter distinguished him from the many minor figures in the history of science whose insights bear no fruit.

The study of fermentation led him to examine similar processes. In 1857, for example, he showed that living agents were at work in the souring of milk. That year he returned to the École Normale in Paris, and for the next thirty years he tackled an enormous range of problems connected with the activities of tiny organisms. At stake there was the age-old puzzle of the origin of life. Were some living things generated spontaneously from non-living matter – or did life come only from life?

Although the frontier between living and non-living is today one of the most exciting fields of scientific inquiry, our controversies are very different from those of a century ago. Spontaneous generation had something of the magical about it: it was a barrier to inquiry. And logically its supporters were at an advantage. A single experiment, perhaps ineptly conducted or misinterpreted, can seem to show that spontaneous generation *sometimes* happens; it is not easy to imagine experiments to show it *never* happens. But in the end Pasteur's experiments satisfied almost everyone that spontaneous generation does not occur under the conditions claimed for it, and the problem of the origin of life was removed from the confusion surrounding it.

Putrefraction, fermentation, souring, and many other processes were all the work of tiny living creatures. Exclude these organisms and their work cannot proceed; control them, as by the cautious heating we call 'pasteurisation' or by soaking in brine or drying in the sun, and their activity will be restricted. In 1864 the implications of Pasteur's work were recognised by the Scottish surgeon Joseph Lister, and by spraying his operating theatre with phenol Lister inaugurated antiseptic surgery. A few years later, Pasteur, although unwell, was himself at work on microbes which he believed must be causing diseases in man and animals.

The first major disease he tackled was anthrax, the scourge of cattle. He showed that the disease was due to living creatures. Chicken cholera experiments later gave Pasteur the vital clue to prevention of anthrax and many other diseases. This discovery of the principle of vaccination caught the imagination of the public and opened the modern era of preventive medicine. When Pasteur died in 1895 he knew that his work had not only added to the store of human knowledge, but had conferred lasting blessings on mankind.

Unlike Darwin, Pasteur is a man of tremendous energy and great emotional drive. Since his middle forties he has been permanently paralysed in the left arm and leg, following a stroke, but he has triumphed over this disability. He has a wealth of achievements to his credit, ranging from the purest of pure science to the most practical problems of technology, and he is held in great veneration, much honoured in his own time and his own country. His indomitable will has been matched by his skill in debate, and he is an accomplished orator in a vein too emotional for Anglo-Saxon tastes. He is a serious and sad man when in repose, kind and thoughtful; though it is not long before the prophetic fires of oratory are aroused in him.

Hoskin: It is characteristic of modern science that when a scientist begins to follow a line of inquiry, there is no knowing where this will lead him. For instance, a problem tackled for its own sake may have the most far-reaching practical consequences. We have a striking example of this in the work of Louis Pasteur.

Pasteur began his scientific career by studying crystals which have certain optical properties – when dissolved they rotate the plane of polarised light. What could be more academic than that? Yet these studies led Pasteur to the micro-organisms that play an essential part in industrial processes like fermentation, and eventually to the germs that threaten the health of man and animals.

And so successful was he in combating these germs that this man, who set out to be a crystallographer, has some responsibility for the population explosion that threatens us all.

Monsieur Pasteur, you have spent the whole of your life in intensive scientific work. You have made great theoretical advances – and you have rescued mankind from some of the most dreaded diseases. Which of these has given you the greater satisfaction?

Pasteur: You cannot distinguish between theoretical and applied sciences. There is science, and there are the applications of science – like the tree and its fruit.

Hoskin: Yes, but I should like to know which aspect of your work gave you the greater satisfaction.

Pasteur: I think, Monsieur, my studies on crystals.

Hoskin: This was the first scientific work you ever did?

Pasteur: Yes, I spent my first ten years in science on crystals – right from the time when I was a young student at the École Normale in Paris.

Hoskin: When did you enter the École Normale?

Pasteur: In 1843, when I was twenty. I had passed the examinations the previous year, but I was well down the list so I felt I ought to wait and take them again.

Hoskin: It sounds as though you were not particularly distinguished at school.

Pasteur: No, I wasn't.

Hoskin: But I've heard stories that you were quite a gifted artist.

Pasteur: Yes, that's true. Here is a portrait I did of my father. He had been conscripted in 1811, and served as a non-commissioned officer. To him the Emperor Napoleon was a superhuman, and he brought me up always to admire that great man and to hate the Bourbons. He was far above his humble position in life. To him I owe everything.

His affection for me was never mixed with ambition for me. Nevertheless I'm sure that some of the success of my scientific career must have filled him with pride. His son – his name – the child he had guided and cared for.

Hoskin: How did you come to work on crystals?

Pasteur: It was a very popular subject at the École Normale, and some of our teachers were leading authorities in the field.

I was in the library one day when I came across a paper by a German scientist in which he pointed out that two particular substances (tartaric acid and paratartaric acid) are in many ways exactly the same – the same chemical composition, the same crystalline forms showing the same angles, the same specific weight and so on. But one of them, when dissolved, deflects the plane of polarised light, whereas the other doesn't.

This seemed very odd – in fact I felt there *must* be some

chemical difference between the two substances. So I prepared the substances for myself, and I examined their crystals closely. Eventually I found that the crystals which deflected polarised light were all orientated the same way, whereas the crystals of the other substance were orientated some one way and some the other.

Hoskin: But we associate your name rather with the study of living things.

Pasteur: My work on crystals led me to the study of microscopic organisms.

Hoskin: This was after you left the École Normale.

Pasteur: Yes. In 1848 I began to teach physics in Dijon, and then the following year I was appointed Professor of Chemistry at Strassburg. It was there that I met my dear wife, who has been my devoted companion in all my work.

But to come back to my crystals. We noticed in my laboratory that certain moulds grow very readily in solutions of calcium paratartrate – one of the substances I had been investigating. Of course we usually threw the stuff away. But it occurred to me one day that the mould might perhaps make some difference to the optical properties of the solution. And, do you know, Monsieur, this is exactly what was happening. The living and grow-ing mould was destroying part of the solution, and this solution was becoming more active optically as the time went on.

My suspicions were well founded.

Hoskin: How lucky for you.

Pasteur: No, Monsieur, in experimental science chance favours the prepared mind. Now, I knew that many substances that are produced by living things have optical properties – and so I came to wonder whether having optical properties might not be the mark of life. I can believe that all living species are primordially functions of the lack of *cosmic* symmetry.

Hoskin: That's something our physicists who talk of the non-conservation of parity would be interested in. But you mean that when you found substances that were un-symmetric, or had optical properties caused by lack of symmetry, you would suspect the action of living creatures?

Pasteur: Yes. In this way I was led to suspect that living creatures might have some part in the fermentation of alcohol.

Hoskin: An important question if ever there was one!

Pasteur: It happened like this. In 1854 I was appointed Professor of Chemistry at Lille, and as such I was expected to take an interest in the industries of the region. I have always been more than happy to go round factories and see industrial processes at work. Well, in 1856 a manufacturer came to me and said that he and his friends were having a good deal of trouble in producing alcohol from beet. To cut a long story short, I discovered in the fermented juice substances that were optically active . . .

Hoskin: And this made you think that there were living processes involved.

Pasteur: Yes. The yeast is actually alive and feeds on the sugar.

Hoskin: Instead of a purely chemical change taking place.

Pasteur: Yes. And the same is true of milk going sour, when the milk sugar is changed into lactic acid. Here again tiny living creatures feed on the sugar. But the problem was, where do these living things come from? Are they germs, carried by the air or already there in the milk? Or are they *spontaneously generated*, simply by the action of the air on the milk.

Hoskin: Now I know the problem of spontaneous generation is a very old one. What does it all mean?

Pasteur: Suppose we have some matter formerly associated with a living being.

Hoskin: A piece of meat, for example?

Pasteur: Yes, but more particularly an infusion in water, broth perhaps, or sugar beet juice. Now, if this substance generates new living beings spontaneously – that is, without help from other living beings – then we say that spontaneous generation has taken place.

Hoskin: If the meat gave birth to maggots, or the broth went bad.

Pasteur: Yes.

Hoskin: This is a pretty fundamental question – the origin of new life.

Pasteur: Yes, it is. But I'm not concerned here with the religious or philosophical aspect of it. I'm only concerned with science. And I don't claim to establish that spontaneous generation has never taken place – in a matter like this you can't prove things *never* happen, and in fact I believe that spontaneous generation may be possible. But I do claim to have given a strict proof that in all experiments in which spontaneous generation has been thought to take place, the experimenter has been deceived.

Hoskin: In other words, you are dealing with what in fact happens in particular cases, as when broth goes bad, rather than dealing with very general issues about the origin of life itself.

Pasteur: Yes.

Hoskin: I can imagine that spontaneous generation would be a very plausible way to explain moulds and things of that sort.

Pasteur: Yes, and as late as the seventeenth century we find Van Helmont telling us how to create mice from flour and soot. But the modern form of the controversy began in the eighteenth century with the work of an English priest called Needham. It was he who first experimented with heating a substance in a closed vessel. He found that if you heated mutton broth and then left it in a closed vessel for a few days it would be swarming with little creatures.

Hoskin: But did he heat the broth long enough?

Pasteur: Not according to his Italian contemporary, Spallanzani. Spallanzani put various vegetable substances in a number of vessels, and then he hermetically sealed the vessels and boiled them for an hour, after which the substances kept perfectly.

Hoskin: What did Needham say to that?

Pasteur: He replied that by boiling for so long Spallanzani had destroyed the vegetative force in the substances – and perhaps spoiled the air in the flask as well; and that this was why no little creatures grew.

Hoskin: Another example of experiments being interpreted in two different ways.

Pasteur: Yes. Well, it would take too long to describe all the work that was done before my time, but I must just mention the investigations carried out by Dr Schwann in Berlin in the 1830s.

It was important to decide whether in Spallanzani's experiments the air in the flask *had* been altered by the boiling, and so Schwann arranged for fresh air to enter the flask after the boiling was over; but he was careful to heat the fresh air before it entered the flask. He found that if he did this there was still no change in the liquid.

Hoskin: But the liquid would have gone bad if the air had *not* been heated.

Pasteur: Yes.

Hoskin: So that the heating of the air had destroyed the germs in it.

Pasteur: Schwann was most careful not to say this – otherwise he would have added a speculation that was not justified by his experiments. All he could say was that there is some principle in ordinary air which causes putrefaction but which can be itself destroyed by heat.

Hoskin: You obviously have to be very careful in interpreting experiments.

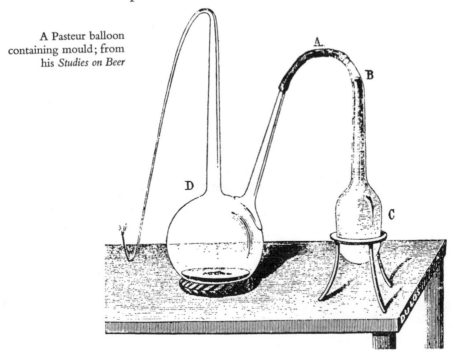

A Pasteur balloon containing mould; from his *Studies on Beer*

Pasteur: And just as careful with experiments themselves; they can so easily go wrong . . .

Hoskin: . . . and you could find yourself spending weeks unprofitably.

Pasteur: Yes, as a matter of fact my dear friend and master, Monsieur Biot, was very concerned when I began this work and begged me to set a limit to the time I would spend on it. But, as I have said, my work on ferments led directly to this problem of spontaneous generation.

Well, my first task was to develop a method for collecting the solid particles that float in the air, so that I could examine them under a microscope. You see, everyone knows that if you boil an infusion of material from living creatures and afterwards expose it to the air, it becomes populated with infusoria or moulds . . .

Hoskin: As much as if you had not boiled the infusion?

Pasteur: No, not so much, because the boiling has destroyed the germs that were already in the infusion.

Hoskin: And so these germs that cause the moulds and infusoria come from the air.

Pasteur: It seems this must be so, and therefore we must try and lay our hands on these germs – find out what they look like, and how many of them there are.

Hoskin: Whether there are enough to account for what happens to the infusions.

Pasteur: Just so. Well, I hit on a very simple technique. I forced the air I wished to examine through a tube with a filter made of gun-cotton. This gun-cotton dissolves in a mixture of alcohol and ether. The fibres of the gun-cotton stop many of the particles, and so all I had to do was to dissolve the gun-cotton. The particles (they don't dissolve) then fall to the bottom of the liquid, and after you've washed them, they're ready for examination under the microscope.

Hoskin: Very neat. What do they look like?

Pasteur: Just like the germs of the lowest organisms, but of course they vary enormously in shape and size.

Hoskin: Are they like those of common moulds, for example?

Pasteur: Indistinguishable from them.

Pasteur

Louis Pasteur in 1884

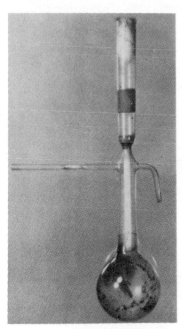

An original Chamberland filter used by Pasteur and
Chamberland for work on anthrax and chicken cholera

Models of crystals prepared by Pasteur in his work on the relation between crystalline form, chemical composition and the direction of rotatory polarization

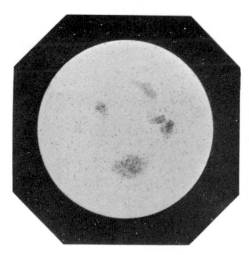

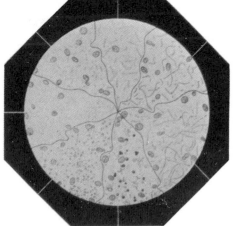

An illustration to Pasteur's studies on diseases in silk-worms: bead-like yeast in mulberry leaf pounded with water and fermented

Illustrations to Pasteur's studies on beer: (clockwise, beginning middle left) turned wine, soured milk, butyric ferment, ropy wine, vinegar, amorphous deposit, sarcinae

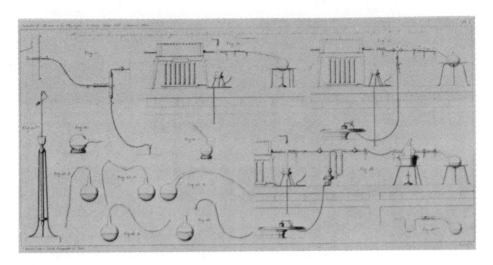

Apparatus used by Pasteur in studies
of air-borne organisms, first
published in 1861

Pasteur's method of observing sealed
culture samples, from his *Studies on Beer*

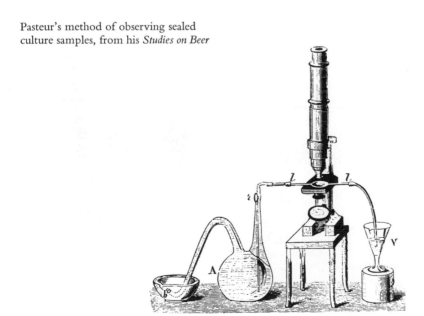

Hoskin: So you knew that the air contains the germs you were looking for.

Pasteur: We must be scrupulously careful: the air contains objects *like* the germs I was looking for.

Hoskin: So what did you do?

Pasteur: At the risk of making it too easy, I will tell you of some wonderfully simple experiments I finally hit on. In a glass flask I would put a liquid that alters very rapidly in contact with ordinary air: yeast-water, perhaps, or sugar-beet juice. Then I heated the neck of the flask and bent it down – like these you see here.

Hoskin: They look like the necks of swans.

Pasteur: Just so. I next boiled the liquid for several minutes, until steam issued freely through the extremity of the neck. This I simply left open. And I allowed the flask to cool. Do you know, you can carry the flask about, let it get warm in summer and cold in winter, and still the liquid will go for years without showing any sign of alteration.

Hoskin: You mean that the particles in the air never manage to get up the neck of the flask and into the main part of the vessel?

Pasteur: I can see no other explanation for these curious results.

Hoskin: But when the flask is cooling, surely the air must re-enter the flask quite quickly, and carry the particles with it?

Pasteur: This is true, but the particles meet a liquid that is still close to boiling point. Later the air enters more slowly.

Hoskin: You mean that by the time the liquid is no longer hot enough to kill the germs, the air is moving so slowly up the neck of the flask that the particles in the air get left behind.

Pasteur: Yes, this must be what happens.

Hoskin: So that if the flask neck is pointed down, the liquid stays pure, but if the flask neck points up, the liquid goes bad.

Pasteur: Exactly. To see this you only need to break the neck of the flask, say after a few months, and, within a day or two, moulds and infusoria will appear, just as usual.

Hoskin: So we know two things. First, that your infusions go bad if and only if the air that reaches them does not have to go uphill; and second, that floating in the air are objects just like the living creatures that make the infusions go bad. But we haven't quite got to the stage of proving that it is these objects that make the infusions go bad – it could be something else in the air, something that brought about spontaneous generation after all. Not a very plausible line to take, of course, but a possible one.

Pasteur: That is perfectly true, and you are right to mention it. But I can point to this liquid and say to you that it is full of the elements suitable for the growth of microscopic organisms. And I wait, and I watch, and I question it. And I beg it to begin anew the first creation – what a beautiful sight that would be. But it is dumb, lifeless, inert, as it has been these many years since my experiments began. And why? Because I have kept it from the germs that float in the air; I have kept it from life, for life is germ and germ is life. Never will the doctrine of spontaneous generation recover from the deadly blow of this simple experiment.

Hoskin: Pasteur was right, of course, but it was many years before his views were universally accepted.

People sometimes say that in science theories only die with the death of those who hold them; but in these questions of such delicacy, involving such tiny organisms, there was every chance of experiments going wrong.

For example, some of his opponents worked with an infusion of hay, in which the germs survived the high temperatures, and so *their* experiments seemed to support spontaneous generation. But Pasteur was now well launched on the study of microscopic creatures, and his later work has proved of untold benefit to mankind. These little germs, once recognised, could sometimes be controlled by heat, as in the pasteurisation not only of milk but also of wine and beer and many other beverages. In human surgery they could be controlled by antiseptics, as Joseph Lister showed. And in due course Pasteur was led to study some of the most terrible diseases in man and animals – even though he himself was by now partially paralysed, following a stroke.

The first major disease he tackled was anthrax, the scourge of cattle. He took a single drop of blood from a sick animal, allowed the organisms in it to multiply in an otherwise sterile fluid, and then he transferred one drop of this culture to another sterile fluid. He did this many times so as to be quite sure that in the final fluid there could be no more than the slightest trace of the original blood. In other words, if this final fluid was harmful it must be because of living creatures in it which had multiplied themselves at every stage of the process. He then showed that the final fluid could kill just as easily as the original blood. In other words, the disease *was* due to living creatures.

Now it had been known for a long time that if you caught cowpox you would be safe from the terrible smallpox; and so doctors gave people cowpox to vaccinate them against smallpox – the very word vaccination comes from the Latin for cow, and, until Pasteur, the word only referred to cowpox and smallpox.

One day Pasteur was studying chicken cholera, and he inoculated some chickens with a culture of the cholera which had been kept for some time. But instead of getting ill, the chickens went on healthily as before. Indeed, when they and some other chickens were all inoculated with a fresh culture, the first batch survived, although the second batch died. Pasteur realised that the first culture had made these chickens immune from the disease – they had been vaccinated. In other words, there was a hope of extending the technique of smallpox prevention to other diseases – as we all know to our great good fortune. Pasteur was amazingly successful in following up this lead with diseases in farm animals, and his public demonstrations became world famous.

But the crisis came when he tackled rabies.

Monsieur, as a boy in the country, you had learned what a terrible death awaits any human being who is bitten by a rabid dog – of course, your first experiments were with animals?

Pasteur: Yes, that's true, although I feel their suffering keenly enough never to have taken up hunting or shooting. If we are to explore the mysteries of life and reach new truth, the end we have in view justifies the means we have to use.

Hoskin: But sooner or later you knew you would have to experiment with rabies in man as well as in animals.

Pasteur: Yes, but with man we must not take liberties. So I began with dogs, and by July 1885 I had obtained no fewer than fifty of them, all resistant to rabies, and I had not had a single failure. Then, on Monday 6 July, three people from Alsace arrived at my laboratory. One of them, little Joseph Meister (he was only nine), had been severely bitten by a rabid dog. The worst of his bites had been cauterised with carbolic acid, but not until twelve hours after the accident, which had taken place on the Saturday before.

That very day I went to the meeting of the Academy of Sciences. There I told two of my colleagues what had happened, and they were kind enough to come and see Joseph at once. They agreed that in view of the number and gravity of the bites the boy was almost certain to contract rabies, and that he faced a horrible death. That evening, with harrowing anxiety, I decided to give Joseph the treatment that I had given to my fifty dogs.

Hoskin: But your dogs had not been bitten *before* you treated them, had they?

Pasteur: No, but I had treated many other dogs in the same way *after* they had been bitten. Well, at eight o'clock in the evening I injected Joseph with material from the spinal cord of a rabbit that had died from rabies fourteen days earlier. Each day after that I gave him either one or two more injections from the spinal cord of a diseased rabbit, but each time with material fresher than the last – and therefore carrying a more virulent form of the disease. I was frantic with anxiety; at night I would dream of Joseph madly suffocating. In the end I inoculated him with the most virulent rabid virus obtainable . . .

Of course by now many hundreds of people have been treated successfully by this method; but I shall never forget little Joseph Meister.

Hoskin: And all this was while you were at Lille?

Pasteur: Oh no, I had returned to the École Normale in Paris long before, back in 1857.

Hoskin: Where you would have better facilities for your experiments?

Pasteur: On the contrary, I had the most miserable facilities, paid for out of prize money and my own pocket. For many years I worked alone; and the flasks with my infusions were kept under the stairs where I had to go on my hands and knees.

Hoskin: In these days a scientist treated like that would soon move to some other country where he would be better treated – the brain drain, we call it.

Pasteur: I have always associated the greatness of science with the greatness of France.

I was once invited to become Professor at Pisa, but I would have felt a deserter if I had gone away from my country in distress to a material situation better than that which France could offer me. In our struggles with Prussia I wanted to see France resisting to the last man. All my work, to my dying day, will bear as an inscription, 'Hatred towards Prussia. Revenge, revenge!'

Hoskin: Then you believe that science should dedicate itself to weapons of war?

Pasteur: Yes, but there are other values that should take precedence. In the present state of modern civilisation, the cultivation of the highest form of science is perhaps even more necessary to the moral state of the nation than to its material prosperity.

I would say to all young scientists, have faith in those powerful and safe methods, of which we do not yet know all the secrets. And whatever your career may be, do not let yourselves be discouraged by the sadness of the times through which all nations pass. Live in the serene peace of laboratories and libraries, until the time comes when you may have the wonderful happiness of knowing that you have contributed something to the good of mankind.

GALILEO

COHEN, I. BERNARD. *Birth of a New Physics.* New York: Doubleday Anchor, 1960.

FERMI, LAURA C. and BERNARDINI, GILBERTO. *Galileo and the Scientific Revolution.* Science and Discovery Series. New York: Basic Books.

GALILEI, GALILEO. *Dialogue Concerning the Two Chief World Systems.* Translated by Stillman Drake. 2d ed. Berkeley: University of California Press, 1967.

GALILEI, GALILEO. *Dialogues Concerning Two New Sciences.* Translated by Henry Crew and Alfonso De Salvio. Evanston, Ill.: Northwestern University Press, 1950.

GALILEI, GALILEO. *Discoveries and Opinions of Galileo.* Translated by Stillman Drake. New York: Doubleday Anchor, 1957.

HALL, A. RUPERT. *From Galileo to Newton 1630-1720.* New York: Harper & Row, 1963.

MCMULLIN, ERNAN, ed. *Galileo: Man of Science.* New York: Basic Books, 1968.

NEWTON

ANDRADE, EDWARD N. *Isaac Newton.* London: Max Parrish, 1950.

HALL, A. RUPERT. *From Galileo to Newton 1630-1720.* New York: Harper & Row, 1963.

NEWTON, SIR ISAAC. *Papers and Letters on Natural Philosophy and Related Documents.* Edited by I. Bernard Cohen and Robert E. Schofield. Cambridge, Eng.: Cambridge University Press, 1958.

SABRA, A. I. *Theories of Light from Descartes to Newton.* New York: American Elsevier, 1968.

WESTFALL, RICHARD S. *Force in Newton's Physics.* London: Macdonald, 1971.

HERSCHEL

ARMITAGE, ANGUS. *William Herschel.* British Men of Science Series. New York: Fernhill House.

DE VAUCOULEURS, GERARD H. *Discovery of the Universe.* London: Faber & Faber, 1957.

HOSKIN, MICHAEL. *William Herschel and the Construction of the Heavens.* New York: American Elsevier, 1970.

LUBBOCK, C. A. *The Herschel Chronicle.* Cambridge, Eng.: Cambridge University Press, 1933.

SIDGWICK, J. B. *William Herschel.* 2d ed. London: Faber & Faber, 1963.

DARWIN

DARWIN, CHARLES. *Autobiography of Charles Darwin.* Edited by Nora Barlow. New York: W. W. Norton, 1969.

DARWIN, CHARLES. *Diary of the Voyage of H.M.S. Beagle.* Edited by
Nora Barlow. New York: Kraus Reprint Co., 1969.

DARWIN, CHARLES. *The Origin of the Species.* Various editions.

DE BEER, SIR GAVIN. *Charles Darwin.* New York: Doubleday, 1964.

EISELEY, LOREN. *Darwin's Century: Evolution and the Men Who Discovered
It.* New York: Doubleday Anchor, 1958.

MOOREHEAD, ALAN. *Darwin and the Beagle.* New York: Harper & Row,
1969.

TOULMIN, STEPHEN and GOODFIELD, JUNE. *The Discovery of Time.* New
York: Harper & Row.

PASTEUR

BULLOCH, WILLIAM. *The History of Bacteriology.* New York: Oxford
University Press, 1938.

DUBOS, RENE. *Pasteur and Modern Science.* New York: Doubleday
Anchor.

NICOLLE, J. *Louis Pasteur.* London: Hutchinson, 1961.

VALLERY-RADO, RENE. *The Life of Pasteur.* Translated by R. L. Devon-
shire. New York: Dover.